for **Placing Children**
in Permanent Families

Hedi Argent

D0785062

Published by
British Association for Adoption & Fostering
(BAAF)
Saffron House
6–10 Kirby Street
London EC1N 8TS
www.baaf.org.uk

Charity registration 275689

British Library Cataloguing in Publication Data
A catalogue record for this book is available from the British Library

ISBN 1 905664 05 2

Project management by Shaila Shah, Director of Publications, BAAF
Designed by Andrew Haig & Associates
Typeset by Fravashi Aga, London
Printed in Great Britain by TJ International
Trade distribution by Turnaround Publisher Services, Unit 3, Olympia
Trading Estate, Coburg Road, London N22 6TZ

BAAF is the leading UK-wide membership organisation for all those
concerned with adoption, fostering and child care issues.

Acknowledgements

I wish to thank all the children, families and professionals I have ever worked with and learned from. Their talents, their generosity, their commitment and their stories have provided me with the material for this book. Names and case studies have been changed only to preserve anonymity.

I am also grateful to Jennifer Cousins, Louise Hocking, Mary Beek and Mo O'Reilly for reading the manuscript at various stages and for their helpful comments.

My thanks also go to Shaila Shah, Director of Publications at BAAF, for her encouragement and for her care in the production of this book, and to her assistant, Jo Francis, who has been ever helpful.

Hedi Argent
October 2006

Note about the author

Hedi Argent is an independent childcare consultant and trainer, and an associate trainer and consultant for BAAF. She is the author of *Find me a Family* (Souvenir Press, 1984), *Whatever Happened to Adam?* (BAAF, 1998), *Related by Adoption* (BAAF, 2004), *One of the Family* (BAAF, 2005), the co-author with Ailee Kerrane of *Taking Extra Care* (BAAF, 1997) and with Jeffrey Coleman of *Dealing with Disruption* (BAAF, 2006), and the editor of *Keeping the Doors Open* (BAAF, 1988), *See you Soon* (BAAF, 1995), *Staying Connected* (BAAF, 2002) and *Models of Adoption Support* (BAAF, 2003). She has also contributed four illustrated booklets to the children's series published by BAAF: *What Happens in Court?* (2003), *What is Contact?* (2004), *What is a Disability?* (2004) and *Life Story Work* (2006) with Shaila Shah.

This series

Ten Top Tips for Placing Children is the first title in BAAF's new *Ten Top Tips* series. This series will tackle some fundamental topics in the areas of adoption and fostering with the aim of presenting them in a quick reference format. Each title presents ten good practice tips, each of which is then further elaborated upon.

Future titles will deal with finding families and managing contact.

Contents

Introduction

This is the book I always wished there was, and finally decided to write myself.

It is not an academic textbook on family placement. Nor is it a comprehensive practice manual for professionals involved in adoption and fostering. It is a kind of elongated checklist to keep at hand for whenever children have to be placed in families away from their birth parents.

I have worked in adoption and fostering for nearly forty years. To begin with, I wanted something easily accessible to reassure me that I was going along the right lines, that I had not overlooked anything vital, and that my agency was being a good enough corporate parent. Later I would have liked a simple handbook to complement the training I was asked to deliver. Now I am hoping to summarise everything I have learnt from the children and families I have worked with, in one slim volume that is relevant to all family placements, is easy to read and will provide triggers for further thought and exploration.

When the title *Ten Top Tips for Placing Children in Permanent Families* was first suggested, it was hailed as a great idea, signalling the start of a new, entirely practice-orientated, series of publications. But the self-doubt that haunts social work soon crept in. Was this title perhaps too trivial? Did it indicate that the book was not serious enough, or even frivolous? There is an uncomfortable feeling that it is not quite professional to concentrate on practice and evidence from experience, and that all social work writing should be directly based on research and quantifiable measurements. There is an increasing danger that "professional" means losing our common sense, and that "practice" will be reduced to ever more forms to complete, and boxes to tick.

This book will not ignore the theoretical side. There are links to relevant research studies and to further reading at the end of each section. But the most important references throughout the text are to the accounts of what works and what does not, and what children and families have said about it. The ten top tips that follow do not cover every topic related to family placement; it would be impossible to incorporate all the information or expertise necessary for placing children outside their birth families under ten headings. But what they do offer is a starting point, a framework, a rough guide, and an aid to learning more.

So perhaps this is, after all, a serious book. I hope it will remind us to approach our basic day-to-day duties in a thoughtful and conscientious way.

> *How we understand the basics, and how seriously we undertake basic tasks, is how we become good social workers.*
>
> *(Louise Hocking, Family Placement Manager)*

Hedi Argent
October 2006

TIP 1
Know the child

> *My social worker is more like a special sort of person. She knows all about my dad and all that and she believes me when I tell her things. It's like she's there for me to see me settled.*
>
> *(Ten-year-old girl waiting for a permanent family)*

If we could walk in the shoes of a child who has to leave home and parents to go and live among strangers, surely one of the scariest things about it would be that nobody knows you: knows what you like and what you fear; what you can do and what you have to struggle with; what you have seen and what you have or haven't understood; what has been lost and cannot be recovered; your place in the family and in your community; whom you love and who loves you. Even as competent adults we can find it hard to start a new job, move to an unknown area, join a class, an organisation or a health club or even to enter a room full of strangers. We easily feel lost, like "a spare part", unconnected to the new environment or the new people. We start to feel more comfortable when we begin to be known. Being known for

3

what we are validates our identity. My family and friends know that I get over-enthusiastic, over-emphatic and over-anxious – in other words, they would say that I'm inclined to "go over the top". I can rely on them to tell me to calm down, but most of the time they accept that this is the way I function. And that makes it feel safe to be me.

If infants have to leave their primary carer, they become disorientated; they instinctively feel unsafe in strange hands, surrounded by unknown smells and sounds. If they could speak they might ask, 'Do these people know how to care for me? Do they know who I am?'

When children, who are no longer infants, are removed from their homes abruptly, the precipitating problems like parental neglect or abuse, family sickness or substance misuse, school exclusion, domestic violence, disability, criminality or homelessness may obscure the child. They are all issues that will have affected the child, but they are not who the child is.

We have to get to know the child before we can make realistic plans. Permanent family placement in kinship care, foster care, or adoption is one of the options that may have to be considered. Far-reaching decisions may have to be made about placing sisters and brothers together or apart. Making decisions about any placement has to be based on knowledge, and knowledge can only come from a holistic assessment relative to the child's age and understanding.

Points to consider

- What were this child's antenatal, birth, and post-natal experiences?
- What kind of attachments have been made and broken?
- Has the developing brain been injured by emotional or physical trauma?
- How does the child deal with rage, shame, impulse and stress?
- Can the child show empathy and trust?
- What is the child's internal model of the world: how does he interpret his own experience?
- Who are the significant people in this child's life?
- What losses and separations has this child endured?
- How has this child developed emotionally, socially, physically, and intellectually?

- Who does this child perceive to be her sisters and brothers?
- What is this child's understanding of the family crisis?
- What is this child's role and place in the family?
- If the child has impairments, how far has he been disabled by his condition?
- What are the child's ethnicity, religion, culture, and sense of self?
- How far is the child's behaviour directly related to events?
- How do other people feel about this child?

If we miss the opportunity to know the child, we will not be able to tell prospective carers who the child really is. Misleading or inadequate representation or a lack of information can lead to the child not being placed or to placements disrupting. The most frequent complaints at disruption meetings come from distressed prospective adopters because the child is not the child they were told about.

> *We thought we'd been told all there was about Jamie, and I still think the social worker did her best, she didn't keep anything from us, but we've found out since that she didn't really know him before she placed him with us.*
>
> *(Prospective adopter at disruption meeting)*

Intending to gather full information and to obtain comprehensive reports is one thing – getting it all done in limited time, and with scarce resources, is another.

Children mostly enter the care system at crisis point when reassurance and protection are uppermost in our minds. But however difficult the situation, invaluable information will be lost if we do not note and record everything we see and hear, because social workers change and memories fade. The police are used to having to make contemporaneous records; social workers are not. Reading through Children's Services files, quotations taken from police records often give the best glimpse of the true picture because they address questions like these:

5

- What did the parents say, how did they look, what did they wear?
- Exactly what happened before, during and after the crisis, and how did the child react?
- How were brothers and sisters and other family members involved?
- How big/small was the home – would a rough plan help to record details?
- Where, with whom and on what did the child sleep?
- What toys, children's books, or clothes were left behind?
- Where was the birth family's home in relation to nursery/school/community – would a simply drawn map be useful?
- Did the child have a special relationship with any neighbours, friends or pets?
- Are any family photographs readily available or can some be taken on the spot?

All children want to hear about "when I was little"; children in care, who inevitably lose so much, must be helped to maintain the minutiae of their own histories, however painful that may be. Parents, siblings, favourite toys, clothes and pets are often equally, but silently, mourned; the memory of places and neighbourhoods may become confused, and many children have recurring dreams of trying to find their way back to their home.

Of course, all this information cannot be collated immediately, but there is always the opportunity to back-track if we know what we are looking for, and it offers a good foundation for getting to know the child and sharing what we know with prospective carers. It also takes time.

> *Understand the child...I know they would have to know a lot about the child. To know a lot about them could really help. Spend time with them.*
>
> *(From Adopted Children Speaking (Thomas et al, 1999, p 140)*

But however much time we spend with children, social workers will never get to know them as well as the people who have lived with them or are living with them now. We have to learn all we can from parents, grandparents, residential workers and foster carers.

Good observation, hearing and listening, attention to detail and careful recording will lay the foundations for good reports; psychological, developmental and educational assessments are needed to fill in the picture. Core assessments and plans for permanence are a statutory requirement but the quality will depend on knowing the child. Social workers need to feel confident that their contribution is pivotal and to be clear about their intended audience; who will read the report – the court, the panel, other professionals, carers, the child now, or in the future, or all of these?

Organising and managing assessments can be frustrating if social workers are expected to identify experts who may or may not have the time to respond. It is helpful for practitioners and their managers to establish a consortium of professionals who specialise in this field, in order to improve and enhance everyone's contribution to the Assessment Framework (Department of Health, 2000). Assessments can be updated as the child progresses, but the sooner they are set in motion, the better will prospective carers be able to "learn the child" and to welcome a real person into the family.

> *Do you know who you are? You are unique. In all the world there is no other child exactly like you. In the millions of years that have passed there has never been another child like you.*
>
> *(From a Jewish prayer to welcome a new child into the community)*

Further reading

Cairns K (2004) *Attachment, Trauma and Resilience*, London: BAAF

Cousins J and Morrison M (2003) *Right from the Start: Best practice in adoption planning for babies and other children*, London: BAAF

Department of Health (2000) *Framework for the Assessment of Children in Need and their Families*, London: The Stationery Office

Fahlberg V (1994) *A Child's Journey through Placement*, London: BAAF

Gilligan R (2001) *Promoting Resilience*, London: BAAF

Howe D (ed) (1996) *Attachment and Loss in Child and Family Social Work*, Aldershot: Avebury

Lord J and Borthwick S (2001) *Together or Apart? Assessing brothers and sisters for permanent placement*, London: BAAF

Lowe N, Murch M, Bader K, Borkowski M, Copner R, Lisles C and Sherman J (2002) *The Plan for the Child: Adoption or long-term fostering*, London: BAAF

Mullender A (ed) (1999) *We are Family: Sibling relationships in placement and beyond*, London: BAAF

Phillips R (ed) (2004) *Children Exposed to Parental Substance Misuse*, London: BAAF

Sroufe LA (2005) *Attachment and Development: A prospective, longitudinal study from birth to adulthood,* London: Routledge

Thomas C, Beckford V, Lowe N and Murch M (1999) *Adopted Children Speaking,* London: BAAF

TIP 2

Work with the child

> *Rina didn't want to make a life story book, or to have a box to keep things in or to do anything else her social worker suggested. But Rina loved maps and she drew a huge map to show all the houses she had lived in and the long and short roads in between. She drew all the people who lived in the houses and wrote their names underneath. Then she decided to stick a golden star on the places and people she liked and a red spot on the places and people that made her unhappy.*
>
> *(From Life Story Work (Shah and Argent, 2005, p 20))*

Leaving home and parents to live with strangers, quite probably with a series of strangers, and then moving again into a permanent family placement, are certainly two of the most unnatural transitions anyone is ever likely to have to make. The first move is often an emergency measure and nearly always due to distressing circumstances, but if permanent family placement is subsequently an option to be considered, a whole package of work with the child will need to be put together before the second major transition.

Aims of working with children

- Children have to make sense of their past, and connect it to the present, before they can look to the future.
- Children have to know how they are going to stay connected to their birth families and to other significant people in their lives.
- Children from minority ethnic backgrounds need to be reassured that their identity will be valued and respected.
- Children need attention and encouragement to tell us their wishes and feelings, their hopes and fears.
- Children have to learn about fostering, adoption, permanence, and finding families.
- Children have to be helped to understand what happens in court.
- Children should be enabled to have an appropriate measure of control over their own circumstances.
- Children have to be prepared to make the next move and to belong to two families.

> *My social worker made me feel I had a real say. He didn't just ask what I wanted all the time, he got me to understand what I could do about it.*
>
> *(13-year-old boy in foster care)*

None of this can be done unless we know the child. And in order to work with the child, we have to be able to communicate with the child. Communication is a two-way process that is agreed upon and understood between people; it may or may not include language but it will certainly include movement, behaviour, and silence. We have to learn how to listen to the silence and how to hear the behaviour. We also have to find out:

- How does the child wish to communicate? Is language restricted?
- If the child is very young, can she understand more than she can speak?
- If the child has an impairment or a learning disability, can we learn the child's communication system? Does the system cover the topics to be discussed, or do we have to find a way to extend it?
- Do we need an interpreter or trusted person to help us to understand each other?
- Should the worker be of similar ethnicity, religion and culture as those of the child?
- How far can/should the current/future carers be involved in the work?
- How long is the child's concentration span? Would it be preferable to "work" for short periods and to spend some time on other activities together? We all know that it is sometimes easier to talk when we are sharing a task with somebody or sitting next to the driver who can't take his eyes off the road.
- Which activities appeal to the child?
  - drawing or painting;
  - play with puppets;
  - listening to music;
  - reading aloud;
  - cooking;
  - board games;
  - car rides;
  - collecting things;
  - gardening;
  - using the computer;
  - taking photos;
  - watching birds;
  - grooming pets;
  - anything else that can provide a safe situation for working together.

It is never helpful to approach the work with a cut and dried plan, because first of all we must engage with the child, and we can only do that by starting from where the child is. We have to remember that every child's experience is unique and requires a unique response. If we have worked successfully with one traumatised child, we must not presume to know what a similar experience means to another child.

Points to consider

Here are ten simple rules for working with children.

1. Try to avoid questions like: 'How do you like school?' 'Which class are you in?' 'What did you do today?' and comments like: 'You've grown since I saw you last'. One bright seven-year-old put an end to that conversation with: 'Yes, I know, that's what children do'.
2. We must accept from the beginning that children in the public care system have been hurt; that some part of them has been damaged. Assume that every child you are going to work with has some deep concern that has never been adequately addressed, like 'Did my father know about me?'
3. We should not avoid distress by asking children about the kind of family they want, instead of hearing their pain about the kind of family they have had. It is more productive to discuss the diversity of families than to raise unrealistic expectations of "forever families" or give the impression that the child can "choose" a family.
4. One of the essential tasks in working with children is to understand how they explain themselves to themselves, and what they understand their situation to be. This touches on their sense of ethnic and cultural identity.
5. Children are not solely interested in verbal communication. They have other means available and we must find out what these are so that we can also use them.
6. We have to be consistent and dependable. A casual 'see you again soon' will not do. Sessions have to be regular and promises have to be kept. We must not add to the child's negative experience of adults.
7. Always meet in a place where the child feels comfortable and establish a routine that suits the child. Routines can be reassuring, special and fun. Including a favourite drink and a biscuit can help.
8. Children need help to develop a true, socially acceptable, logical explanation of their own story. Without it, children frequently

resort to fabrication and run the risk of being labelled a liar.

9. We must commit ourselves to a multi-faceted view of the child. Everyone who has contact with the child will see something slightly different. There is no one right way to experience another person.

10. We are not only communicating with the child, but we must also be able to convey a true sense of this child, and the child's history, to future carers and other professionals and in reports we will have to write.

(Adapted from *Opening New Doors* by Kay Donley (BAAF, 1975, out of print))

Working with children is usually described as life story work or "direct work" because so much of what we do in child care is done outside this one-to-one relationship. With increasing requirements to meet targets, to complete forms and to comply with new legislation, there are ever-greater demands on our limited time. Working with children, who are not usually clamouring for it, can easily be cut short, delegated to the least experienced workers or left to foster carers. It is true that foster carers probably know the child best, but they should not be expected to get on with it by themselves. Joint working, like any co-operation between adults, can be both reassuring and healing for disorientated children. If joint work is not feasible, each session could end by sharing progress with the carer or the social worker.

Quinton *et al*, in their 1998 follow-up study of children in permanent placements, found that unfocused direct work offered no benefits. Agencies might do well to have a designated, specially trained worker, or perhaps an accessible play therapist, to act as an adviser and consultant on life story work with children.

A child's life story is a never-ending story. Life story work is more than putting a chronological narrative together in a book, and it is also not the same as a photograph album with captions. Life story work is a process which enables children to make sense of who they are, and why they are where they are, and to understand where they might be going. Children's lives become fragmented when they live with different people in different homes; the aim of life story work must be to put their lives together again with space for the future. And life stories need not be confined to a book: a collection of mementoes in a box, a scroll, a wall-map, a shield, a flow-chart, or a website and any number of imaginative diagrams like family trees, genograms and family circles can illustrate a child's life. The most important thing is that the life story book, or its equivalent, is owned by the child and created by the child, with however much help and stimulation from adults as are needed. It is advisable to make duplicates of precious materials for safe keeping with the child's records.

> *Experiment with your own life story. Draw a tree with roots to represent birth family, community, environment, ethnicity, and religion. You can be the trunk. Each branch is a stage in your life and the leaves bear the names of the people you remember. There are strong branches and weak branches. Some are intertwined and some reach out on their own. The tree is still growing; there will be more branches and if some leaves drop off, others will appear. How will the tree get rain and sun and good earth to remain healthy and safe? Is there a rainbow in the sky? Or thunderclouds? What happens if the wind blows and storms rage? What is in the world around the tree?*

When young children have to leave their birth families, some of their memories get lost because they are separated from the people who hold their memories for them. Very few of us really remember much of what happened to us before we were three, unless it has become part of our life story. I know that when I was 18 months old, I stood in the middle of our garden with the hose full on, scared and unable to put it down. As successive members of the family tried to rescue me, I turned towards them and gave them a thorough soaking. I only know I did that because I heard the story told over and over again.

We cannot collect all their memories for children when they enter public care, but we can at least make sure that they do not lose any more. A "memory book" can be held for every looked after child and passed from carer to carer. In it should go all those anecdotes about what has happened only to this child in this way: the funny things she said, and clever things he did, and how she got lost, and he fell into the duck pond – all this is part of a life story, and of life story work.

It is never too late to find more information for a child. If parents are reluctant or too angry to provide histories and photos, aunts, uncles, and grandparents may be more obliging. Or you and the child can travel down memory lane together, taking photos and talking to relatives, friends, neighbours, teachers and previous social workers and carers.

> *Liam's single mother died when he was six. He saw her carried away in an ambulance. She just disappeared from his life, and because he had learning difficulties and never asked, he was never told what had happened to her. He lived in children's homes until he was 11 and was about to be placed for adoption. The only life story work that interested Liam was to hear about his mother. Then he wanted to learn about death and dying and funerals and cemeteries. A social worker took him to find his mother's council grave. He started to collect money to buy her a gravestone, and when he moved to his adoptive home, his new parents helped him to realise his wish. The birth mother's gravestone became the cornerstone for the adoptive relationship.*

Older children may lose memories that hurt too much to hold on to. They will need expert help to recover and to process them; this goes beyond the bounds of ordinary life story work and should initially be left to therapists who specialise in working with children in transition. Later on, with the support of their therapist, the child can control how to incorporate painful facts and feelings into their life story.

> *Tracy was 12 years old. Her father was in prison for injuring her baby brother. Tracy told everybody that he had left home because he was so upset when her brother was sick and died, and that's what she wrote in her life story book. Tracy saw a psychotherapist three times a week. After one year she told her social worker that she wanted to write something new in her book. This is what she wrote: 'I hate my dad for hurting my brother and it was me called 'help' from the window 'cause there was blood everywhere and my mum was out of it and I hate them both.' Tracy had much more work to do with her therapist but she was beginning to put her story together.*

It is not the end product but the process of life story work that matters.

● Because it is now obligatory for every child to have a "life story book" when moving to a permanent placement (Adoption Agencies Regulations 2005), there is a danger that well-presented, neat books will become the aim; or that a life story book will be regarded as the sole purpose of working with children.

  ◆ One enthusiastic new social worker got a ten-year-old boy to write everything out in rough, and she then typed and printed sheets to stick into an expensive album, with mounted photographs to illustrate the text. It was a beautiful piece of work and was praised and appreciated by the adopters who took great care of it, but it had little meaning for the child.

  ◆ Another boy of the same age arrived in his adoptive home with a roll of white wallpaper, which he unfurled proudly to show his new parents how far he had come to find them. The scroll was full of roughly cut out, stuck in pictures, smudges and spelling mistakes; it had been torn and mended with sellotape, but it provided an opportunity for the child to explain himself, and for the family to listen. In due course more was added and it became part of his continuing story.

- No child is too disabled to have a recorded life story. Seven-year-old Kevin, who could not speak or walk, enjoyed signing every page of his book with differently coloured handprints. When he moved, he would not be parted from it. Although he could certainly not comprehend what it was, he knew it was his; he tore all other books but not this one. He turned the pages carefully, pointed at the hands, and laughed.

- All children who have to separate from their birth family are going on a journey. If they are disabled, and many children placed from care have a disability, it is an extra factor to take into account when designing each child's package of travel information. Even if they cannot ask, they may be concerned about the answers to some of these questions:
  - Do I need another family because I am disabled?
  - Are there other children like me? What happened to them?
  - Will they know I can't walk? Will they be strong enough to lift me? Will my wheelchair go in?
  - Will they understand me when I speak "funny"? Will they know sign language?
  - Will they cope with my fits? Give me my injections?
  - Will they have rails in the bathroom? Help me to dress?

  And the ultimate question:
  - What happens if they can't manage like my birth parents couldn't?

  These concerns are also part of their life story.

- If children are resistant to working on any kind of tangible life story record, it does not mean that they don't want to do life story work. Perhaps they need time to sift through memories and information before they are ready to commit themselves to any specific version of their own story. That process will be more significant than whether they want to make a book or anything like it. And a book or anything like it is only a small part of life story work.

Profiles

A "profile" has come to mean a brief description of a child for publicity purposes. Whenever possible, depending on age and ability, each child should be actively involved in contributing to their profile and in the plans to publish it. Writing a profile should not be a one-off event to meet a deadline in a magazine. It has to be part of the preparation work for permanent placement.

It is important for children to know that profiles are a way of telling families about themselves and not like "advertisements" for best buys. Children should be able to say what they want a family to know about them and to decide how they want to describe themselves. It is more interesting to read: 'Jamie says he is quite nice sometimes', than the often seen adult comment: 'Jamie is a happy boy'. Children may also want to ask readers something, like Jamie did: 'Ask them if they've got room for a rascal', he said to his social worker.

Nothing should go in a profile unless a child, who is able to communicate and understand, agrees. This might take more time and more work, but it will be time well spent because a reluctance to complete a profile may indicate that a child is not ready to be placed in a new family. However, Steve was very clear about what he wanted and he wrote it himself: 'I don't want to say anything about me but I do want to have a new family'. He got a big response from intrigued prospective adopters, his family-to-be among them.

Children should also be involved in the follow-up to publicity as part of the ongoing "direct work". Teachers and carers should be alerted to give extra support during this time. If an information pack is sent out, the child should see one. If several people enquire, the child needs to know: 'What happens next? How long will it take? How will you choose? When do I meet them?' If there is little or no response, the child needs to know that we will try again; that if we haven't found a good enough family, we haven't tried hard enough.

Thirteen-year-old Darren was featured in a national newspaper. He wrote most of his own profile and, although usually a low-spirited boy, he felt sure he would find a family this way. His social worker failed to warn him that boys of his age often have to wait a long time because he didn't want to dampen his enthusiasm. There were only a couple of enquiries and the social worker didn't tell Darren about them in case they came to nothing. When they did come to nothing he was glad he hadn't raised Darren's hopes, especially as Darren had withdrawn into his shell again and didn't ask any questions. Soon afterwards the social worker left. The next worker wanted to try more publicity but Darren refused. It took many sessions of careful work with Darren to persuade him that he was not "rubbish", that two families had asked about him, and that next time, or the time after that, the right family might turn up.

(From Profiling Children (2002, p 4))

Further reading

Argent H and Kerrane A (1997) *Taking Extra Care*, London: BAAF

Barn R (ed) (1999) *Working with Black Children and Adolescents in Need*, London: BAAF

Gilligan R (2001) *Promoting Resilience: A resource guide on working with children in the care system*, London: BAAF

Morris J (2002) *A Lot to Say*, London: Scope

Quinton D, Rushton A, Dance C and Mayers D (1998) *Joining New Families: A study of adoption and fostering in middle childhood*, Chichester: John Wiley and Son

Ryan T and Walker R (1999) *Life Story Work*, London: BAAF

For children

Argent H and Lane M (2004) *What Happens in Court?*, London: BAAF

Argent H (2004) *What is a Disability?*, London: BAAF

Argent H (2004) *What is Contact?*, London: BAAF

Foxon J (2001) *Nutmeg Gets Adopted*, London: BAAF

Foxon J (2002) *Nutmeg Gets Cross*, London: BAAF

Foxon J (2003) *Nutmeg Gets a Letter*, London: BAAF

Foxon J (2004) *Nutmeg Gets a Little Help*, London: BAAF

Foxon J (2006) *Nutmeg Gets into Trouble*, London BAAF

Kahn H (2002) *Tia's Wishes*, London: BAAF

Kahn H (2003) *Tyler's Wishes*, London: BAAF

Shah S (2003) *Adoption: What it is and what it means*, London: BAAF

Shah S (2003) *Fostering: What it is and what it means*, London: BAAF

Shah S and Argent H (2006) *Life Story Work: What it is and what it means*, London: BAAF

Useful resources

Alton H (1987) *Moving Pictures*, London: BAAF. A book with pictures to talk about and colour in.

BAAF (2002) *Profiling Children*, Practice Note 41, London: BAAF

Betts B and Ahmed A (2003) *My Life Story,* CD ROM, Information Plus. Seven interactive sections with printable worksheets, music, sound and colour animation.

Callam R, Cox R, Glasgow D, Jimmieson P and Groth Larsen S (2005) *In My Shoes: A computer assisted interview for communicating with children and vulnerable adults*, York Child and Family Training.
(Available via training course only: liza.miller@btinternet.com)

Camis J (2001) *My Life and Me*, London: BAAF. A life story book that can be adapted for any child. Guidelines for creative use are included.

NSPCC Powerpack (2001, 2006), London: NSPCC. Providing information for children and young people involved in public law proceedings.

TIP 3
Find a family for *this* child

If permanent family placement is the plan after holistic assessments based on knowing the child and working with the child, then finding the right family for *this* child has to be the next or concurrent task. When family placement, adoption or fostering teams become involved, it is vital that they work closely with the worker who knows the child.

- **There is a family somewhere for every child that needs one.** If we haven't found the family, we haven't looked hard enough. Almost everyone can be a parent for some child or children, but hardly anyone can be a parent to any child.
- **Keeping the child in the birth family has to be the first option.** According to legislation, guidance, and common sense, it is best for children to grow up in their own families unless it is unsafe for them to do so. Kinship carers, including close friends, have the advantage of knowing the child, of sharing the family history (probably also the ethnicity, religion and culture), and of having an investment in keeping the family together. Kinship care builds on existing attachments and family strengths, and makes continuity for the child a reality. Enabling kinship carers to come

forward requires pro-active work with the whole family. Family Group Conferences (FGCs) offer a useful model and are discussed in more detail under Tip Number 8. (Extensive information about FGCs is available from the Family Rights Group – see Useful Organisations.)

- **Children will get placed if social workers believe they can be, and should be.** It's easy to give up if any of the workers are dubious about the aim or feasibility of the placement plan, or find that no applicant fits exactly what they have in mind for "their" child. Workers need to be totally committed to finding a family. Very few people make perfect parents, but most of us manage to be "good enough" parents; with decent preparation and training, permanent carers are no exception.

- **Every child deserves an individual recruitment campaign.** A profile in a magazine may not be enough, even if repeated over several months. It is preferable not to rely on any one item of publicity before trying another. Tailoring a campaign around each child's needs will take more time but produce more viable possibilities sooner. Alternatively, a bigger campaign can be mounted to serve a small group of children with similar needs.

> *Three infants with Down's syndrome were referred to the same agency at the same time. An area with good services for disabled children was identified and targeted. Leaflets with photographs and brief profiles were placed in every doctor's surgery, library, religious and community centre. The local media were sent information packs and an open meeting was held in the Town Hall. All three children were placed in the area and the three families formed a support group.*

- **Advertising or featuring a child?** Featuring children in special magazines and the local and national media is purposeful publicity; talk about "advertising" children is demeaning for the child, the birth family, and the prospective carers; it also misleads social workers into "selling" the child as though it were a competitive market. At worst this results in profiles that vie with each other to present the child as the most desirable, thereby making unique children sound alarmingly alike.

- **Much good publicity comes free.** Local radio stations and newspapers are always interested in "human" stories and are usually eager to support children. Links with journalists can produce articles in magazines to find a family for a specific child and some features may merit a mention in editorials. Letters to journals and newspapers can create interest in the special needs of a specific child.

Letter to Farmer's Weekly

Dear Editor

Rosie has always dreamed of living on a farm. She wants to look after animals and "grow things". She hopes the country will be quieter than the town she lives in.

Rosie is six years old; she can't live with her birth family and needs parents (one would do), who will want to adopt her. Rosie is very good at helping and says, 'I like working nearly all the time'. But Rosie doesn't like leaving her immediate surroundings and will need help to go to school and make friends with other children.

If any of your readers want to know more about Rosie, we would like to hear from them.

Marion Davies

Adoption Team

Telephone: 000 0000

● **It doesn't matter how many or how few people respond to publicity.** One family is enough if it is the right one. Sometimes workers feel discouraged if they have made a great recruitment effort that produces little or no choice. Having a wide field to choose from does not necessarily mean the right family has been found; it may be a reflection of an unrealistic profile or of placement workers trying to find children for their approved families. Families are off to a flying start if they have been encouraged to respond to individual children rather than waiting to have children suggested to them.

● **"Approved" families should not necessarily be given preference.** It may mean more work for hard pressed social workers, but training, assessing and preparing a family with a specific child in mind can lead to sounder placements. It is hardly possible to prepare a family adequately for "a child under three with mild learning difficulties". Many placements have floundered because a child under three with mild learning difficulties did not meet expectations. It may be much more effective to help families to consider the impact Jade will have on them, and how they might meet all of Jade's special needs. Jade is two-and-a-half and her development is delayed, but age and ability are only two narrow aspects of a complex little girl.

● **Single carers, unmarried, lesbian or gay couples, and disabled carers, can make "first choice" parents for "first rate" children.** It must never be a question of lowering sights, but of widening our horizons. There are no second-class children and there can be no second-class parents. No one has a right to foster or adopt children but everyone has a right to be given the opportunity to be considered as a permanent carer. Many children thrive in the one-to-one situation that single parents can offer; family patterns are changing and "partners" are becoming as common as "husbands" and "wives"; lesbian and gay carers may be best equipped to bolster a child's self-esteem and resilience, and disabled parents can be inspirational models for us all.

- **Recruiting black and dual heritage families requires extra effort.**

> *I think losing, you know, your birth family, your parents, and your country and community and culture and everything, and people don't think it's very relevant because you've never known it, and so I don't think people think you have a right to actually grieve any of that.*
>
> *(Intercountry adopted adult quoted in In Search of Belonging (Harris (ed), 2006, p 129))*

It is not enough to feature a child in a regular magazine and to write, 'He needs a black or dual heritage family'; or to say, 'We are looking for a family that can reflect and promote the child's ethnicity and culture'. Different publicity may have to be devised, expert workers may have to be involved or consulted, links with faith or community groups may have to be explored and cultivated (see Rule, 2006). We have to learn about the meaning of fostering and adoption in different cultures. Members of minority ethnic groups would surely come forward more readily if a higher value were placed on what they have to offer.

The arguments for "same-race" placements have been generally accepted, addressed in National Standards, and enshrined in most local authority policies. There should be more compelling reasons than not easily finding a matching family if a transracial permanent placement is to be pursued.

> *Not some effort, but every effort should go into finding a match. This takes greater strength of commitment rather than a longer period of time. Token gestures carry an expectation of failure.*
>
> *(Louise Hockney, Family Placement Manager)*

However, some questions about children from minority ethnic backgrounds will not go away. How long can a child wait for a "matched" family? And how matched is matched, considering the wide diversity of African, Asian, African-Caribbean and mixed heritages? And if half-siblings have different minority ethnic backgrounds, is it perhaps more important to find one family that can deal with diversity, rather than several "same-race" families? If a deliberate decision is made to compromise, then there must be a clear understanding of the qualities the family will need, and the support they will be given.

- **Many of the children who need families today have physical, mental, or sensory disabilities.** Disabled children of all ages need new permanent families. In a recent survey of children referred over a three-month period to *Be My Parent*, the BAAF family-finding newspaper, Cousins (2006) found that 40 per cent had an impairment or some special need that could affect placements. This figure does not take into account the children with deep emotional scars. Disability is therefore not a marginal issue in family finding.

> *It has now been shown that children who in the early 70s would have remained in residential care, in hospitals, or in residential special schools can be placed with families who not only want them, but also grow to love them and enable their development and fulfillment beyond the expectations of social workers in the past*
>
> *(Wedge and Thoburn, 1986, p 78)*

- People may choose to adopt or foster a disabled child because they are "into disability"; they have a disabled family member, a disabled child already in the family, a professional connection, or a religious motivation.
- Publicity in special schools or hospitals, short break schemes, residential homes or the specialised disability press may all be fertile ground for recruitment campaigns.

- Having experience of disability is not a prerequisite. It is also necessary to engage the general public.
- Some families who have brought up their own children successfully want to go on being parents and are ready to take on different challenges from ordinary parenting.
- Prospective carers may rule out taking a disabled child if the focus is on the disability rather than on the child.

If we can introduce the whole child before we focus upon the extra needs, we are already overcoming one of the major barriers. A recruitment drive to enlist more carers for disabled children may therefore work best if the images on the posters show a variety of children, some with visible impairments, some with none – all having fun together. If existing carers of disabled young people can participate in campaigns and address meetings (the so-called "horse's mouth"), so much the better. In fact, we need to integrate disability issues into all our work: make it part of the mainstream.

(Cousins, 2006, p 28)

- **Welcoming applicants in, rather than weeding them out, can find more families for more children**. Even if Mr and Mrs Brown are clearly not the right parents for Jane, they might turn out to be the best for Michael.

Sue and Brian Brown came to the office in response to a feature about five-year-old Jane who had lost both parents in traumatic circumstances. It was an emotional response and they quickly realised they wouldn't be the right family for her. But they saw a poster about Michael, who was 15 and wanted a family to see him through school and into college. They fell for him, and were reassessed specifically for Michael. It was a lovely placement but we would never have thought of them, and they would never have thought of Michael if we hadn't invited them into the office.

(Social worker from a voluntary agency)

Putting prospective carers into a category at the approval stage does not inspire creative placements. Sue and Brian had been approved for a child between the ages of five and eight.

* It can be self-defeating to make too many prescriptions when seeking new families. Especially for older children, it may be wise to focus on permanence, and to leave the door open for either fostering or adoption. Some people want only to adopt, others would much rather foster; what children need is to know that they will not have to move again; care plans will have to meet the requirements of either the Fostering or Adoption Regulations.

* Saying that a child must be the youngest or only child in the family and that she needs two parents could rule out at least half the interested families, and the right one may be among them. The child's position in relation to the carers' own children will depend on individual family dynamics, and will have to be thoroughly explored as part of a later assessment.

* Envisaging that contact will have to take place X number of times with this and that person, puts a negative slant on continuity; contact arrangements will work better if they are negotiated rather than imposed.

* To state that families will have to be loving, patient or energetic is surely stressing the self-evident. It is much better to stick to describing the child as truly and as fully as possible, to state what support will be available, and to wait and see who responds and what they can offer.

* We have to believe that prospective carers are most often good judges of what they can and cannot do – that they

do not want to take a child whose needs they could not meet, or a child who would not fit into their own family.

- **Prospective carers need to know if and why siblings are being separated.** It can be upsetting to read that siblings are being separated. Being told that they have special or different needs won't do; all children have special and different needs. Further explanations are necessary.

> *Margaret read about two severely autistic deaf brothers, aged six and eight, who, it was said, needed to be placed separately, each in a two-parent family, because they had to be closely supervised and physically restrained. It happened that Margaret was a teacher at a school for deaf children and had brought up her own autistic son. She now lived alone in a large house in a supportive community. She felt strongly that these two brothers should stay together, and persuaded their local authority that she could manage if given enough support. With the help of generous grants and a rota of paid and volunteer workers she managed very well. She adopted both boys, and organised their move to fully supported independent housing when they were in their early twenties.*

Most studies have found that being placed with at least one sister or brother has a stabilising influence on long-term placements. When siblings have to be separated there is an association between regular contact and good outcomes (Rowe *et al*, 1989).

If a large sibling group is to be split up because it is thought that no one can take so many children, then this ought to be plainly stated: there just might be someone out there who says, 'I'll take them all if you help me'. And that might include help with housing and transport as well as allowances and guaranteed access to appropriate children's services if and when needed.

● **It is essential to devise a quick and comprehensive response to every approach from potential carers.** New enquirers can easily be put off by too many initial questions, and experienced applicants may go elsewhere if they are given inadequate information.

> *An experienced foster carer enquired about a child featured in her local paper. She was handed from one person who wasn't aware of the feature to another who clearly knew nothing more about the child. The carer withdrew.*
>
> *(From Profiling Children (BAAF, 2002, p 3))*

Would-be carers complain that it is difficult to get hold of the right person, that social workers don't always reply to messages, and that administrative staff are not properly briefed to deal with enquiries. But it need not be so.

> *Every time we phoned we spoke to Mark's social worker or to the secretary who knew us and she would always take a message. We were told straight away, the first time, that we weren't too old and that more information would be sent that same day and it was. We were never kept hanging on or waiting for a call. It made us feel they knew what they were doing. It wasn't a bit like we'd expected.*
>
> *(First-time adopters)*

Good publicity will only be as effective in finding families as the follow-up service an agency can offer.

- Does everyone in the department know about the publicity when it appears?
- Are other workers briefed to take a call if the key worker is not available?
- How far can administrative staff contribute to the immediate response?
- Is the information culturally sensitive?
- Is there an information pack ready to be sent out?
- How soon can all enquirers be invited to an open meeting or to an initial interview?

Feeling valued at this stage will help families to appreciate the purpose of training, assessment, and preparation that will follow.

Further reading

Argent H and Kerrane A (1997) *Taking Extra Care*, London: BAAF

Broad B and Skinner A (2005) *Relative Benefits: Placing children in kinship care*, London: BAAF

Cousins J (2006) *Every Child is Special: Placing disabled children for permanence*, London: BAAF

Harris P (ed) (2006) *In Search of Belonging: Reflections by trans-racially adopted people*, London: BAAF

Macaskill C (1985) *Against the Odds*, London: BAAF

Mallon G and Betts B (2005) *Recruiting, Assessing and Supporting Lesbian and Gay Carers and Adopters*, London: BAAF

Rowe J, Hundleby M and Garnett L (1989) *Child Care Now: A survey of placement patterns*, London: BAAF

Rule G (2006) *Recruiting Black and Minority Ethnic Adopters and Foster Carers*, London: BAAF

Wedge P and Thoburn J (eds) (1986) *Finding Families for "Hard-to-place" Children*, London: BAAF

TIP 4

Prepare a family for *this* child, and the child for *this* family

Even if families have already been approved to foster or adopt, the most important part of the family placement process should be related to a particular child, preferably a child followed up by the family from basic information. Some carers say that initially it has to be 'like falling in love', and 'then you can deal with the difficulties when they come'. Others talk about an immediate curiosity about one particular child – 'it was like she jumped out of the page at us, and wouldn't let go'.

If prospective carers are not yet approved, more of the assessment and training can be tailored around the needs of a specific child or group of children and how the family might, or might not, have the commitment and competence to meet those special needs associated with the child's development and circumstances. The task is to assess, and to help potential carers to assess, how this child will impact on this family, and how this family will impact on this child. In most cases the child's worker will not be the key worker for the family, but joint work will help the family to consider the child's needs in relation to their own. It is helpful to think of this stage as "linking" a child with a family and to use the term "matching" only after the compatibility of this child and this family has been assessed.

Because children cannot make life-changing decisions and choices on their own behalf, the adults, both carers and professionals, bear a double responsibility for achieving stable placements. Effective training, assessment and preparation will be intertwined and on a continuum from application to placement. Agencies will have their own procedures for working with prospective carers, but it is vital never to curtail the part of the work that deals with *this* family's preparation for *this* child.

> *We thought we were all done once we were approved, we thought that was all that mattered. We never expected so much more to happen when we went ahead with Jody. It was a real eye opener hearing what other people saw in her, and how she was tied in with her birth family. It made us think about her and us, like you couldn't when it was going to be any little girl. We spent days and days seeing her social worker and foster family and going to her school and talking it all through with our own social worker before we ever met Jody. It was worth every minute we spent. When she came to live with us, we didn't have any surprises.*
>
> *(Permanent foster carer)*

It is not only the prospective carers who have to be prepared for Jody or any other child. The carer's existing children will certainly require attention, and grandparents-to-be as well as other relatives or friends who will be involved in supporting the placement could be included in some form of preparation. Two useful techniques might be considered.

1. **A Child Appreciation Day** can be a means of sharing a great deal of information in a relatively short time. It is a day for prospective permanent carers to meet all the people who have known or worked with the child. It creates an opportunity for a multi-faceted view of the child to be shown, which can be illustrated by videos, photos, anecdotes and facts. The agency's medical, educational and legal advisers should be present for at least part of the day; less official people may also be able to make a significant contribution – Jody's new family, above, met her favourite school dinner lady and the foster carer's neighbour, whose own daughter was Jody's regular playmate. Social workers should produce visual aids on flip charts: family trees and family circles, and flow charts to represent moves, separations and losses can sometimes communicate more than words. A Child Appreciation Day could be described as a guided journey through the child's life, which must always be mindful of how the child sees it. Such a day works best in a friendly, spacious room with comfortable chairs arranged informally. Drinks, biscuits and sandwiches for lunch are usually very welcome. As Jody's family put it, 'That day gave us the chance to put the questions we didn't even know we wanted to ask'.

2. **A Family Meeting** may be a good way of helping the prospective carers to include their families in their plans. Many grandparents have said that they could have done with some input from social workers but didn't like to ask because the process was taking such a long time anyway, and their children were already stressed. Getting the family on board in time can be a factor in making a placement work.

> *My son and daughter-in-law told the social workers about all the relatives that were interested and would like to help. We had a meeting at our house and they said about how the children would be and they explained why, and what we could do to help.*

> *Having three big children come into the family like that, all at once, was different for us and for their aunties and uncles as well. And there were ten cousins waiting for them. The older ones were chuffed at the idea of thinking up ways to make them welcome.*
>
> *(Parent of prospective permanent carers)*

It is possible that during this intensive process families will discover that they cannot, after all, become the right parents for this child or group of children. It will be less painful for all concerned if they withdraw now, than if the placement disrupts later. Every stage of the road to permanence ought to offer the choice of going on or calling a halt.

Ethnicity, culture and religion

Presumably, families and children will have been as carefully linked as possible, and the child's needs for an ethnic and religious match will have been balanced against all other needs. It is then easy to overlook the diversity within a "match". If this child and this family share the same religion, how different are the customs and practices they observe or ignore? And how far will the family introduce the child to their own way of worshipping, assimilating or remaining separated from mainstream culture? Will the ethnicity of the child be submerged in the family's "nearly the same" background, and how would that matter to this child and to this child's birth family? And can carers who may have lost their country, their people and their communities help this child to deal with the loss of a birth family?

> *One continuing theme that emerged…concerned the carers' own personal grief resulting from their separation from, and loss of, their country of origin and extended families. This is not to suggest that such an experience prevents black and minority*

> *ethnic parents from becoming "good enough"*
> *parents. On the contrary, it can be of positive*
> *benefit if they are able to explore and manage their*
> *own feelings of loss. An important task, therefore,*
> *was to...identify strategies for dealing with*
> *emotions that might be triggered for them by caring*
> *for very hurt children.*
>
> *(Duck, 2003, p 149)*

While we may be equipped and prepared to consider the impact of ethnicity and religion, we might be more reluctant to confront the issue of class. Attitudes to education and health, work and leisure, food and drink, manners and discipline, are embedded in every family system. And family systems reflect class and community values as well as ethnicity and religion. It is not essential for this child and this family to share every attribute; indeed, it is unlikely that many would, but it is important to be aware of the differences and what they might mean for this placement.

Information and confidentiality

If people are expected to take total responsibility for a child, then it is only common sense that they should be entitled to have all the available information about that child. Information for permanent carers should never be censored but always be supplemented by someone who knows the circumstances, someone who can separate fact from opinion and put the record in context.

If carers do not have access to the child's files, they must be able to trust that nothing relevant is being withheld. If they are able to read the files themselves, they will need to discuss the implications of what they have read with the child's worker and their placement worker. In inter-agency placements it is essential that the family's worker has read the child's records before the link is finalised.

Families, like the children themselves, will need help to decide what is confidential and what can be shared with others. Children have a right to privacy; all the details of their often tragic stories do not have to be told to neighbours, friends, or even new relations, although teachers and doctors may need to know more. Families have to be warned how hard it can be to be blamed for their child's behaviour by other parents who do not, and should not, know the whole history, and how seemingly insensitive other people can be.

> *...it can become seriously annoying that often well-meaning neighbours, some of whom I have barely spoken to before, keep commenting on the adoption. Do they not realise that a boy of Peter's age can comprehend a lot of what is being said? As a close friend observes, when you adopt a child you seem to become "public property". First there are questions and assumptions regarding your infertility, and then very personal questions about your child's history and background. 'So where did he come from then?' left me incredulous. Just as infuriating was: 'When do you think you'll adopt another?' as if everything in life were that simple – and as if we'd picked Peter off a shelf. I have to remind myself that for a lot of people, adoption is a bit of a mystery, something that is talked about a lot, but little is known about. Therefore, it is understandable that people are curious to find out more.*
>
> *(From An Adoption Diary (James, 2006, p 102))*

Exchanging life stories

During the final stages of preparing an identified family for a specific child, when the family has confirmed its commitment, life stories may be exchanged. This is the time when the child will first learn that a family is waiting. She or he will already have worked on a life story and produced something to send to the prospective carers. The family should now be given time to collate information and photos to introduce themselves to the child. Videos and audio recordings may be welcome but should be used with care; it can be overwhelming for a child to be faced with too much too soon. A tape with a song or piece of music sent as a special communication may be more meaningful and less threatening.

At this point children ought to be encouraged to ask all the questions they can think of about their "new family". Children may want to write notes to the family to ask questions directly, or they may want their social worker to act as a go-between. Some children and families have established a regular correspondence before formal introductions begin. 'What time will I have to go to bed?' wrote one seven-year-old, and the reply came, 'How does eight o'clock sound to you?'

Some of the important questions are more difficult to ask. It can be helpful to role-play question and answer sessions; giving the child a turn at being the parents may elicit hidden yearnings or reveal suppressed fears: *Shall we go fishing together?* or *I won't get cross if you wet the bed.* The social worker, as the child, can find words to say the impossible: *How can I trust you to love me?* and *Do I have to love you?*

Factors leading to good placements

- Sufficient and clear information for prospective carers before a match is confirmed. The most common complaint at disruption meetings is that the family did not know, were not told, or were not helped to understand what they read.
- Easy communication with, and between, all the workers involved – inter-agency placements require special care in this direction.
- Giving time. Too often there is a sense of urgency as soon as a match has been made. The stage of preparation for this child should be acknowledged as the most vital part of the process.
- The child's readiness to move. The best-prepared family will not make the placement work if the child is not ready for the transition. It may be better to wait and plan further work with the child.

- The family's eagerness to locate schools, health and support services to meet the needs of a particular child.
- A striving for "openness" rather than "open placements", leading to a workable plan for continuity and contact (see also Tip 9).
- The promise and delivery of agreed and continuing post-placement support (see also Tip 7).
- And finally: just as 'Good fences make good neighbours' (Robert Frost [1874–1963] *The Road not Taken*), so do 'Good assessments make good placements'.

Further reading

Argent H (2004) *Related by Adoption: A handbook for grandparents and other relatives*, London: BAAF

BAAF (1999) *Assessment, Preparation and Support: Implications from research*, London: BAAF

Barker S, Byrne S, Morrison M and Spencer M (1999) *Making Good Assessments: A practical resource guide*, London: BAAF

Cousins J (2003) 'Are we missing the match? Rethinking adopter assessments and child profiling', *Adoption & Fostering,* 27:4, pp 7–18

Duck M (2004) 'Working with black adopted children and their families: the Post-Adoption Centre's experience' in Argent H (ed) *Models of Adoption Support*, London: BAAF

James M (2006) *An Adoption Diary*, London: BAAF

TIP 5

Use introductions to listen, hear, and observe

> *I catch my breath as I have the first glimpse of our son standing at the foster carers' front door – a beaming smile etched on his face, his hand waving madly.*
>
> *It is two pm on Tuesday afternoon and we are due to go to the park with Peter and his foster carer…We are supposed to act as naturally as possible, while introducing ourselves as Peter's new mummy and daddy!*
>
> (From An Adoption Diary (James, 2006, p 82))

How does it feel to meet your new parents for the first time, to be introduced to your son or daughter, to let go of a cherished foster child, to see yourself as a discarded birth parent, or to be responsible for a match that must carry the risks inherent in all family placement work? During the final stage before the move to permanence, all these emotions will be brought together under the umbrella of "introductions".

And because it is the final stage, it will also be a tense stage; there may be voiced or unspoken exhortations to "speed up", to "go slow", to "lighten up", to "show more commitment", to "keep to the plan" or to be "more flexible", depending on who is putting on the pressure. This is the time to take stock, to ensure that everyone concerned is heard, and to also hear what is not said.

The purpose of introductions

Whatever the details, every introduction plan has to have the aim of supporting the child and the adults, while the child moves from one set of carers to another.

It is perhaps useful to begin with a pictorial idea of what the introduction plan is supposed to achieve. Imagine a seesaw. Before introductions start, the child and the current carer(s) together weigh down one end of the seesaw, and the prospective carer(s) are up in the air on the other end. As introductions progress, the child will move nearer and nearer to the centre of the seesaw and eventually the carer(s) will hover equally balanced on either side. At this point the child will need full support and encouragement from both sides to remain upright. When the child is ready to make the move towards the new family, the balance will gradually change again, until the weight of the newly combined family makes their side of the seesaw go right down and takes the current carer(s) up.

Introductions ought to enable the child to make the difficult move from one side to the other; and anyone who remembers trying it on a real seesaw will know how hard it is to do this without falling off. Thinking about the seesaw can help us to start introductions from where the child is, and demonstrating on a diagram could be a way of getting the planning meeting off to a good start.

One aspect of the transitional process, which may be overlooked in the effort to put the focus on the new relationship, is that the withdrawal of the current carers ought to be as gradual and as measured as the introduction of the new family. Several agencies have a policy whereby the first stage of introductions is conducted in and around the home of the current carers, and a second stage takes place in the new family's home, with the current carers' involvement slowly diminishing.

> *Although we have a couple of successful outings to nature reserves and parks, as well as an award-winning tantrum in McDonalds, when Peter flings himself on the floor like a starfish, both Robbie and I are keen to be back on our own home turf...*
>
> *Peter does not seem unduly concerned by the foster carers leaving him at our house; he probably realises he will see them later on...*
>
> *We collect Peter every morning from the foster carers' rented cottage...In the middle of this second week...it is decided that Peter will move in with us for good in two days' time. The foster carers will come in for a quick cup of tea, some last minute photos and then they will leave for their journey home.*
>
> (From An Adoption Diary (James, 2006, pp 83–87))

Peter's introductions were complicated by distance and by the limited understanding of a three-year-old. Even so, the arrangements allowed him to balance between both families until he was as ready to make a move as he could be in the circumstances.

The length of introductions

The proverbial piece of string is a fitting measure for introductions. Two children of the same age, and with apparently similar histories, may not be able to take introductions at the same pace. So much will depend on the quality of the relationship with current carers, on previous transitions, on the preparation work, on the initial response to new carers, and on everyone's inner timescales. One child will want to burst into the new family circle, while another will be much more cautious; one foster family will let go more quickly than another, and prospective carers may be the sort of people to make an instant commitment or to take it step by step.

There is no one right way or a one-fits-all length of time for each age range. It may be true that older children need longer and more spaced out introductions, and that it is best for very young children to have intensive, brief introductions because they cannot conceptualise what is happening, but every plan will need to be tailored to very individual needs and circumstances.

Introductions offer an opportunity to "practise" becoming a family, and by the end of introductions everyone should feel confident enough for that final leap forward. How long it takes to get to that point is less important than what happens along the way.

Asaf was seven years old and had lived with his foster carer for two years. He wanted a family of his own but he found all change difficult. His prospective adopters were prepared for lengthy, drawn-out introductions. The plan was to visit Asaf in his foster home, and for his carer to bring him to visit his new family on alternate weekends over a two-month period. Then there would be a review to assess progress and decide how to proceed. In between weekend visits, the prospective adopters sent postcards and telephoned. Sometimes they spoke only to the carer, who then relayed messages to Asaf, and sometimes Asaf sent a message to them. After five weeks Asaf asked to stay the night in the room he had helped to get ready in the new

> *family's house; he stayed and his carer stayed too. He left some of his toys there "for next time". The review was put forward and it was agreed that Asaf was ready for the next stage. Two weeks of almost daily visits followed with weekend stays in the new home – the first one with, and the second without, Asaf's carer. At the end of the second week Asaf moved in permanently.*

Asaf's introductions were led by his difficulties in dealing with change rather than by a formulaic timescale for a seven-year-old. The introduction plan was clear and purposeful enough to make Asaff and both sets of carers feel confident, but also flexible enough to meet changing needs.

The timing of introductions

Birthdays or Christmas and other religious or cultural festivals are not good times to be separating a child from a family where routines and rituals are familiar and eagerly awaited. It is understandable that prospective carers are keen to share a big Christmas tree or a birthday outing with their child-to-be, but it will be better for the child not to confuse such occasions with introductions and for the new family to create other special occasions and enjoy different outings together.

Children often make gifts and cards at school for their families at special times and birthdays are usually marked in some way. It is important to be aware of what is going on in the child's world when introductions are planned.

> *Eleven-year-old Lily was distraught when she was told that she would miss the last day of school before half term. The class had been working on a "Black British" project, which was to culminate in a*

> *carnival parade and she would have to miss it when she went to meet her new family.*

Foster families also have a legitimate interest in minimising the disruption to their own families when a foster child leaves. If a planned, imminent celebration has to be abandoned, it will not encourage the foster carers to support the new placement.

The beginning of the long school holidays is another trap to avoid when placing older children. It can be beguiling to imagine shared lazy summer days and exciting trips, but many children settle more easily into a daily routine that includes some respite at school from the emotional demands of relating to a new family. And the new family may also do better if they have the opportunity to recharge their batteries regularly. Biological parents often complain about the long holidays and their bored children; adopters and foster carers and family placement workers, please take note.

That is not to say that every child should be bundled off to playgroup, nursery or school the moment she arrives in a new placement. Most children will need time to absorb one change before they are ready for another, but placements have disrupted because six weeks of unbroken and rising tensions have proved too heavy for the child or the new family.

We also have to be careful that adult agendas do not get in the way of focusing on the child's interests. Introduction plans can be heavily influenced by work and holiday schedules or by other family commitments.

> *Ellie, aged six, lived with her foster family for two years until a single adopter was found. The match was approved at the beginning of July. Her foster family was due to go on a booked holiday abroad at the end of July. The local authority decided that Ellie should not go on this holiday with them because it would intensify*

her bond with the foster carers at the wrong time. The social workers wanted introductions to be completed before the holiday. The prospective adopter, a professional woman, had always made it clear that she had to give one month's notice to get adoption leave. She could not begin introductions until the beginning of August. Ellie was moved to a "bridging family" while the foster carers went on holiday. She was introduced to her prospective adopter while her foster carers were still away and her regular social worker was on sick leave. She went back to the foster family while introductions continued. She hardly had time to show her rage at having been deserted by them, before she moved into her "forever" family, which was not forever. The placement disrupted after six months and Ellie moved to yet another short-term foster home.

Ellie's introductions could serve as a blueprint of how not to do it; Ellie's needs were overshadowed, for perfectly understandable reasons, by the agendas of all the adults.

Making the introduction plan

Here are some simple guidelines that could be followed in every case.

- The lead person, who will chair the initial planning meeting and review, will need to maintain independence when amendments to the plan are proposed – as they inevitably will be.
- The plan has to enable the child to move; familiarisation to a new family and a new place will require different strategies for each child. Disabled children may have to be introduced by touch, smell and taste as well as sight or sound.

Natalie was blind. Her prospective carers always wore the same clothes and watches and jewellery during introductions; she wore the same perfume and he used the same after-shave lotion. They always brought the same audiotape to play to her and when introductions transferred to the new home, the clothes and smells and sounds came too. Natalie moved more easily than many sighted children because the familiarisation had been so carefully planned.

- The plan has to be negotiated and agreed by all parties; it won't work if arrangements are imposed. It may be a great idea for prospective carers to turn up in the foster home in time to get their son-to-be up at six in the morning, but it won't help the child if the foster carers consider it an intrusion.

- The plan has to be realistic and manageable; distance and where people can stay have to be carefully considered. Prospective permanent carers will be tense enough without having to worry about travel arrangements in the rush hour or uncomfortable accommodation.

- The plan has to be constantly monitored and possibly adjusted; not everything will work out exactly as planned. Everyone has to know which worker will be available when, who will liaise with whom after every meeting, and who will be supporting the child, the current carers, and the new family.

- The plan has to include a mechanism for hearing what everyone, particularly the child, is saying or finding it too difficult to say; unforeseen problems, cold feet, or risks observed have to be taken seriously. Many foster carers complain that they had reservations about what they saw going on during introductions, but that their views were not heard.

- The plan should be formally reviewed at the half-way stage and again before placement; it is never too late to postpone the move if the child is not ready, or if the prospective family is having second thoughts, or if the agency is having doubts about proceeding. If introductions do not lead to a placement, it will be sad for all concerned but less sad than a disruption later. It is very hard for social workers to interrupt or end the placement during introductions without strong support from their manager.

> *Satwant was introduced to an experienced "same-race" family when he was ten. He had cerebral palsy, used a wheelchair, and had lived most of his life in a residential home for disabled children. He was an intelligent boy with good communication skills, although sometimes hard to understand. Introductions went well and according to plan until Satwant spent a night in the prospective carers' home. He said he hated the new bed that had been specially bought for him. No amount of reasoning or cajoling would persuade him to spend another night in it. The move was postponed while the agency tried to make sense of what was happening. The carers became disheartened and decided that they would not be able to cope with what they saw as controlling behaviour. Once Satwant was assured that he would not have to move, he asked whether the prospective carers could become his special friends – other children in the residential home had "independent visitors". Satwant's clear message that he was not ready to move was heard and acknowledged. The prospective carers became his "independent visitors" and got to know him well enough to understand that he was scared rather than wilful. Two years later they adopted him. They joked that they had the longest introductions in childcare history.*

Further reading

Byrne S (2000) *Linking and Introductions*, London: BAAF

James M (2006) *An Adoption Diary*, London: BAAF

TIP 6

Maintain and monitor continuity for the child

Connection, continuity and contact are the three components of "keeping in touch". We are all connected to other people, communities, places and countries; we all require continuity in our lives if we are to function as integrated beings. In order to remain connected and maintain continuity, we may, or we may not, need or wish to have contact with certain people, to revisit certain places and to observe certain rituals and traditions.

> *The loss of my birth mother through adoption has meant the loss of my birthright: of a way of life within the Indian community; of a rich and beautiful*

49

> *culture; of knowledge of my maternal history and ancestry; and of my ability to speak my mother tongue...*
>
> *(Shobha (2000) quoted in Harris, 2003, p 129)*

Hardly anyone today would suggest that children can or should make a "clean break" when they move into permanent placements, however traumatic their past experiences have been. It is not a question of whether children should remain connected to their birth families, but rather how continuity can be preserved and how children can be protected in problematic circumstances. Staying connected can mean anything from keeping absent people in mind to direct face-to-face contact.

Ways of staying connected

1. Unsupervised face-to-face visits, outings, special occasions.
2. Direct: telephone, email, texting, postcards, letters, photographs, videos, audio recordings, presents.
3. Indirect letterbox: exchange of letters, cards, photographs, possibly presents, through a named third party, usually the placement agency.
4. Supervised meetings.
5. Memory boxes, life story books or alternatives, address books, photo albums, maps.
6. Clothes, food, cultural observances.
7. Keeping absent people in mind by creating rituals to remember them.

It is common practice when children have to separate from their families of origin to make immediate contact arrangements; quite often these arrangements are imposed by the courts or by departmental policy. There is, of course, no doubt that children should retain active links with their birth families, especially as only a minority will remain looked after on a long-term basis (Milham *et al*, 1986), but in the rush to make arrangements for a suitable location, to agree frequency, and to determine who should be involved, the purpose of contact can be overlooked.

And there is sometimes a danger that contact arrangements can become bargaining counters in care proceedings without reference to the purpose of contact.

Purpose of contact

1. To keep children's lives intact by maintaining continuity with the past.
2. To maintain existing relationships.
3. To build relationships for the future.
4. To help with long-term identity issues.
5. To provide models of co-operation.
6. To avoid fantasies of all-good or all-bad fairytale parents.
7. To enable children to overlap their family circles and integrate their life experiences.

Points to consider

- **The practice of "goodbye visits"** with birth family members has to be questioned if we accept that adopted children will always be the children of two families. And children may blame the new parents for having to say "goodbye" to the old.

> *I believe there is no such thing as "termination" in the relationship between children and their birth families. Even if the birth parents die, it's not "over". By creating a ritual based on a pretence that the relationship has ended, the child's internal reality is at odds with the external one.*
>
> *(Pavao, 1998, p 97)*

- **Children may freely love many adults** if the adults have a positive regard for each other, but they will find it much harder to maintain positive emotional ties with adults who are hostile to each other.
- **The preparation and support for keeping in touch** are vital

elements of the work with children, birth families, carers, and adopters.

- **We have to be aware that "keeping in touch" can have different meanings for different families**. Depending on the family system, it could mean sending birthday cards once a year, or living in each other's pockets; "phoning occasionally" might mean every week or twice a year. We have to make sure that we are communicating effectively when we negotiate contact arrangements. **Written agreements** can help us to make sure that everyone knows what everyone means.

- **It is difficult to challenge contact arrangements directed by the courts,** but we have to be allowed to find workable ways of maintaining continuity for each child when permanence plans are made. And then we have to define the purpose of contact for each child with each person, before the arrangements to serve that purpose can be agreed. A clear exposition of how a contact plan will be formulated should satisfy judicial concern. A cut and dried plan is more likely to deal with the quantity than the quality of contact.

Having been told that the permanence plan for ten-year-old Sandra was fostering because she retained strong and positive links with her birth family in spite of a history of abuse, the judge, on the Children's Guardian's recommendation, ordered supervised contact with various relations four times a week. The local authority was hard pushed to find the resources to supervise so frequently, and the permanent carers were apprehensive about the disruptive effect on Sandra. The birth relatives were resentful about being supervised and frequently didn't turn up, which upset and angered Sandra. The purpose of contact was unclear to all concerned.

- **When a child is placed for permanence, it is as well to wait**

and involve the prospective carers in negotiating contact arrangements to meet their new child's needs. Whatever is envisaged at the planning for permanency stage should be open to further discussion with the child, if appropriate, and with the new carers and the birth family. If the purpose of staying connected and continuity can be agreed, the arrangements will follow more easily.

- **Most foster carers have a significant part to play in helping a child to maintain continuity during the transition to permanence.** The more attached to them the child is, the more urgent it will be for them to stay in the picture. They can be the best people to reassure the child by co-operating with the new parents, by demonstrating that you don't have to break relationships in order to make new ones, and by providing active links between past, present, and future. Far from preventing children from settling, continuing direct contact with previous carers can enable the child to settle more comfortably. Foster carers may need training to understand why this is so important to children, and they will need support if contact is upsetting as well as rewarding for them. Children who have already sustained many losses should not be exposed to more unless absolutely necessary for reasons of safety.

- **If children are distressed by contact** it may be necessary to review the purpose and the arrangements, but it is rarely an indication for abandoning continuity. It is hard for adults to witness a child's distress, and it may be tempting to see the solution as cutting off from painful situations, but it might be better to work with the child to deal with it.

- **Good contact arrangements for siblings** are not only related to the number of possible visits but depend on how far contact enables the children to share their lives.

This nostalgia of theirs is extraordinary, each of them feels the richness of it. On and on they'll talk: a whole afternoon will disappear while they take turns comparing and repeating their separate and shared memories and shivering with pleasure every

> *time a fresh fragment from the past is unearthed.*
>
> *(Shields, 1995, p 175)*

- **Even if telephone or letterbox contact are fairly meaningless for very young children**, it is important to incorporate them into the adoption story, and to keep letters in a special folder until children are old enough to understand. Older children can be encouraged to participate in the letterbox arrangement and to decide what to say and what to send to their birth family. Research has established that very young children, who do not have a complex relationship with their birth parents as a result of early experiences, usually manage face-to-face contact as a normal part of the "getting to know people" routine. If the adults build links, the children will be able to draw on them when they are older and more aware of their adoptive status (Neil, 2002). As one adopter said, 'It's much like keeping up with your own relations – sometimes it's good and sometimes it isn't, and it stops the birth mother becoming a stranger'.

- **What is needed in order to maintain continuity will change as circumstances change**, and as children grow older. A three-year-old cannot remember people he does not see frequently; a ten-year-old can keep people safely in mind. If a very young child has had only letterbox contact, she may be curious to see her birth parents by the time she is 10. A teenager may want to cut off entirely from the past, or a young adult may yearn for a reunion with his birth mother. Families may move, change partners, have other children, and become less available. And children in the same permanent placement may need different ways to keep in touch. Rigid plans for continuity, even when the purpose is clear, are less likely to meet the changing needs of individuals than more flexible arrangements, and access to a means of reviewing contact.

> *Dawn and Arleen were sisters placed for adoption aged two and six. There was direct contact with both birth parents twice a year. Arleen looked*

forward to her mother's visits but said she didn't want her birth father to come because he favoured Dawn. Dawn had no conscious memory of her parents; she regarded them with interest, from a distance, like any other visitors.

By the time Arleen was 10, friends, school and family activities took up all her time and she became uninterested in her birth family, just as Dawn, now aged six, was beginning to understand the significance of having two families and asked to see her birth parents more often.

The birth parents separated, moved far away, and lost touch with the sisters when they were in their teens. Arleen was angry with them and swore she would not see them if they ever turned up again. When Dawn was 18 she began to trace her birth mother and hoped for a reunion.

The same family also adopted Alan when he was seven, and three years younger than Dawn. Alan had letterbox contact only with his mother and grandmother because it was considered unsafe for him to see any member of his abusive family.

His adoptive parents helped Alan to keep his absent family in mind. Alan wanted to meet his birth mother when he was 15. The adopters persuaded the local authority to arrange a meeting and stood by while Alan met his birth mother on his own. He wanted to ask her about his early childhood but made it clear that he did not want to have an ongoing relationship. They reverted to letterbox contact.

> *The adopters were supportive throughout and regarded continuity as one of the factors that made all three adoptions work even when there was no face-to-face contact.*

- **As well as maintaining continuity for children, we also have to protect them from further harm.** Our increasing knowledge of the impact of trauma on a child's developing brain must alert us to the risks of both direct and indirect contact for babies and small children; indeed, for a child of any age, their history of abuse may make any further contact dangerous or prevent recovery. 'If you came from hell, wanting to experience a bit of heaven before you look back isn't too unreasonable, is it? (Smith, 1995, p 97). But even in such cases, children have to look back in the end to own their past. Safety is not the same as severance.

> *Sue and Bertie were terrified that their parents, who had caused them to be abused by a paedophile ring in exchange for drugs, would come and find them in their new and permanent foster home. They were reassured when the judge made an order forbidding the parents any other kind of contact than Christmas cards during the remainder of their childhood. Only then could Sue and Bertie begin to remember the good times, and make a start on their life story work.*

- **Supervised contact may be necessary in some situations**, but we have to be quite clear what we mean by supervision, and why it is necessary, and who will do it. Is it for the child's safety? Is it to support the carers or the birth family? Is it to assess relationships? Is it to prevent inappropriate behaviour? Or is there a lack of confidence about the purpose of the meetings? Should supervision take the form of discreet observation, active participation, or high-level scrutiny? And should carers ever be put in a supervisory position?

- **If arrangements for maintaining continuity cannot be agreed with the parties concerned, it may be helpful to use a mediation service.** Mediation can support both the birth family and the permanent carers in negotiating arrangements within parameters that would be acceptable to the local authority and to the child. It should enable everyone to speak and to be heard without fear of being persuaded or put down. If possible, the mediation service should include a child advocate to represent the child's wishes and feelings (Plant, 2006).

- **Disabled children have as much right to, and need of, continuity as other children have.** Birth parents of disabled children may need a great deal of sensitive support if they feel unable to stay in touch or feel it is best for their child if they do not. Even if children cannot express a wish for contact or show pleasure when it takes place, the loss of continuity is a further handicap, which must be avoided.

> *It could be argued that a child with learning disabilities can only make sense of her world if the relationship with her birth family is maintained, or a child with physical impairments can only accept himself if his birth parents also accept him.*
>
> *(Argent, 1996, p 3)*

- **Keeping absent people in mind** is what most of us do at some time or another. We remember Uncle Ned in Australia, even if we haven't seen him for years and hardly ever write, because we tell stories about him, send him birthday cards, and keep him firmly in the family circle. We can help children to keep their birth family in mind by creating rituals and stories for the purpose. One adoptive family held hands, and blessed their adopted children's birth parents before every birthday celebration; another opened up a diagram of their family circle to let the birth mother in, and they pinned the drawing up on their family notice board.

Contact from the child's perspective has to be the first thing to be taken into account when decisions are made about sustaining continuity. As in every aspect of family placement work, the child's interests have to be paramount, and the child's interests can only be served by trying to "see as the child sees", and learning how the child feels about "keeping in touch" – contact is not a word a child will often use. It may be that older children refuse contact even when everyone else supports it.

> *Maria feels strongly that she has always been let down by her mother and is angry now about her mother's marriage. At this time Maria needs to put her energies into her new family and should not have any contact unless she wishes to have it. However, Maria is just 12 years old and it is not possible to predict what her feelings and wishes will be as she gets older. It will be vital to monitor what those feelings and wishes might be, and to ensure continuity now, by incorporating her life story into the new family's narrative.*
>
> *(From a Children's Guardian's report)*

Children past infancy can tell us who is important to them and who is not; they know who their brothers and sisters are, although we may not understand how half-siblings they have never met can figure so significantly in their lives. A "eurocentric" view of families must not prevent us from appreciating the richness of cultural diversity. Birth grandparents or other relatives may be more important than birth parents for some children: one boy of six collected granddads as he went along; he retained one by birth, three from foster families and he found a new one in his adoptive home. He wanted to know: 'How many granddads am I allowed?' Grandfathers were his passport to continuity.

Further reading

Argent H (1996) Practice Paper *Post Adoption Services for Children with Disabilities*, London: Post Adoption Centre

Harris P (2003) 'Am I alone in my grief? User support for transracially fostered and adopted people' in Argent H (ed) *Models of Adoption Support*, London: BAAF

Macaskill C (2002) *Safe Contact? Children in permanent placements and contact with their birth families*, Lyme Regis: Russell House Publishing

Milham S, Bullock R, Hosie K and Haak M (1986) *Lost in Care: The problems of maintaining links between children in care and their families*, Dartington: Dartington Social Research Unit

Neil E (2002) 'Managing face-to-face contact for young adopted children' in Argent H (ed) *Staying Connected: Managing contact arrangements in adoption*, London: BAAF

Pavao JM (1998) *The Family of Adoption*, Boston: Beacon Press

Plant D (2006) *Contact from the Child's Perspective*, London: Post Adoption Centre

Rushton A, Dance C, Quinton D and Mayes D (2001) *Siblings in Late Permanent Placements*, London: BAAF

Shields C (1994) *The Stone Diaries*, London: Fourth Estate

Smith G (1995) 'Do children have a right to leave their past behind them?' in Argent H (ed) *See you Soon: Contact with children looked after by local authorities*, London: BAAF

TIP 7

Agree a support plan for this placement

Support means feeling cared for, being listened to, and being able to have a bit of a grumble without feeling criticised.

(Permanent carer in O'Neill, 2003, p 16)

It is the accepted wisdom that good support is an essential component of successful family placements. But what exactly does that mean? When and how often do children, carers and birth families need support? How much and what kind of support do they want and how can they get it? Is peer group reassurance as valued as professional expertise? How can support be evaluated and measured? And do social workers and families perhaps have different perceptions of what is helpful?

Giving and receiving support are part of the same communication process. But what is offered with the best of intentions by the provider may not always be experienced as supportive by the recipient.

> *Unless a mother is completely off the wall, she knows what her child needs and doesn't need. Like an electric wheelchair; someone once thought that Adam should have one, but I thought, whatever do they think he's going to do with it?*
>
> *(Single adopter in Argent, 2003, p 171)*

Adam had multiple disabilities and was very limited in what he could do. The well-meaning social worker, undoubtedly concerned about the daily management problems faced by his adoptive parent, had offered the most expensive and up-to-date equipment available without a proper awareness of how it might, or might not, help this particular family. Another permanent carer wished that her social worker would ask what she needed at different times: sometimes she just wanted encouragement, sometimes it was counselling, and sometimes it was practical matters, but she didn't like 'to keep asking for new things'.

As a starting point, we should perhaps acknowledge that support can only be as good as it feels, and that the same package of support will feel different to every child and family. And if it feels good enough at one stage, it may not feel as good at another.

Points to consider

- Some children want to have someone to talk to who is outside their two family circles, but some children definitely do not.
- One foster carer may be well satisfied if her supervising social worker visits once a month to discuss progress and problems, while her friend, who also fosters, may need to talk to the same social worker on the telephone for half an hour every week, to recharge her batteries.

- One family will appreciate meeting with other permanent carers in a group, while a second family, in similar circumstances, will feel that they have enough troubles of their own and do not want to hear about any more.
- What is plenty of money for one person is not enough for another.
- Permanent carers may expect to have short breaks when they need them and ask for them, or they may prefer to plan a year ahead.
- Adopters can be pleased to host reviews in their home after adoption, or they can find them intrusive.
- One family will take complicated matters of health and education in its stride, but red tape and procedures will overwhelm another.
- Some permanent carers will welcome the opportunity to manage and maintain contact arrangements with birth families; many would perceive it as an unwelcome responsibility if left to get on with it.
- Birth families (see also Tip 8) may reject all offers of support unless tailored to their individual needs, but this does not mean that they do not want to be supported.
- Having a support worker from their own ethnic group may be important for some families but not for others. Cultural competence will be important for all.
- And finally, what feels like support to some people can feel like supervision to others. We have to be very clear and careful about which we are offering.

Practice issues

Support for permanent placements has been enshrined in current legislation, regulations, National Standards, and guidance (for details see *Adoption Now* and *Fostering Now* under Further Reading at the end of this chapter). Foster Placement Agreements and Adoption Support Plans are intended to cover present and future needs and provision. Although the requirement for assessments of needs is very clearly spelt out, the duty to provide is a little less specific, and care has to be taken when plans are made to define what will actually be offered, and how, and by whom. It is intended that provision will be shared with education, health, housing, and any other relevant services.

An Adoption Support Services Advisor (ASSA) now has to be appointed by every agency (in England and Wales; new Scottish legislation is to come) to give advice to other professionals, to act as a point of contact for all parties to adoption, and to promote and maintain agreements at a strategic level across departments and agencies. There is no such mechanism for planning and review in foster care, but good practice would suggest that a foster care services manager carries similar responsibilities.

Placement support should never be tacked on as an extra at the end of the placement process. Discussions about the kind of support that might be needed, would be expected, and could be provided in each particular case are an integral part of preparation, assessment, and training, and should also inform adoption and fostering panel recommendations. The official guidance suggests that assessments should follow the Assessment of Children in Need and their Families Framework and that needs should be met by mainstream provision whenever possible. This is not necessarily a comfortable fit: the framework is not family placement sensitive, and placements could be put at risk by delays and waiting lists or by lack of family placement expertise.

> *We joined our local Association and went along to their meetings but they all thought we were weird for having adopted Sam when they were all struggling with having children like that born to them.*
>
> *When Sally needed speech therapy the waiting list was that long, it was no use to us.*
>
> *Then when we didn't agree about the boarding school, we had to tell the social worker from the disability team that we didn't adopt Sam just to send him away again.*
>
> *(Adoptive parent of two children with disabilities)*

There is a further possible debate about who should assess support needs and arrange for provision. The child's worker will be familiar with the *Assessment Framework*, and the child's background, but may be less knowledgeable about transitions to permanent placements; the ASSA should be most experienced in networking and involving other agencies, but may not even have met the child or the family; the family placement worker will have the best overview, but may not be used to the *Assessment Framework* or to contracting out to other organisations. The solution is clearly to work together on each assessment and ensuing support plan, but this has resource implications that have to be accepted at a policy level.

Financial responsibility for foster placement support rests with the foster carers' agency at all times, but in the case of independent fostering agencies, local authorities will be charged for the service. If children and adopters are represented by different agencies, financial responsibility is divided according to regulations (see above).

Elements of placement support

- **Accurate, appropriate information along clear and reliable lines of communication.** Children, permanent carers and birth families have to know who will be doing what, how, when and for how long. They have to trust that relevant information will be updated and shared with them. New regulations, benefits, legislation or medical discoveries may affect placements now and in years to come.
- **Inter-agency and inter-departmental liaison and co-ordination.** When more than one agency is involved in a placement, inter-agency agreements have to cover every possible eventuality. It can be very disconcerting for carers to feel that one agency doesn't know, or approve of, what the other one is doing. "Splitting" between agencies or departments can lead to mutual blaming that can only get in the way of dealing with difficulties in the placement. It is never helpful to have "good guys" and "bad guys" in placement work.

Belinda, a single prospective adopter, was extremely well supported by a specialist agency, whose workers were available at all times. When the placement of a five-year-old boy began to run into serious trouble, she complained that the local authority, responsible for the child, was not giving her enough practical or financial help. Instead of getting together immediately with the carer, the two agencies started to question each other's practice and the carer was left to "take sides".

Maria and Tom fostered and adopted three children with a diversity of special needs. They were visited by teachers from their children's schools, by at least three social workers, by a home chiropodist and dentist, by a benefits officer, by a health visitor, and by volunteer helpers from a local charity. Some days two or three "experts" would call on the same day. The family felt inundated by unco-ordinated support. They needed and valued the help they were getting but Tom said, 'There's a lot of overlap and it's left to us to sort it out, and we don't have any time just to be a family'.

A post-placement worker might help effectively by convening an annual meeting of all the professionals involved to listen to the carers, and to plan a continuing, comprehensive joined-up service together, for the following year.

- **Counselling for the adoptive family and for the birth parents.** Needs will vary as the child grows up and family dynamics change. A seemingly trouble-free infant placement may become more problematic when the child reaches puberty or adolescence; a birth family may struggle with grief after many years. Post-placement workers can act as sounding boards and mirrors whereby families measure progress. They should also be trusted to sound the first alert if they notice something going wrong. It is no help to think, let alone say, 'I saw this coming', when it is too late.

- **Direct work with the child.** Working with children who have had to separate from their birth family does not stop when the child is placed with a permanent family. Hopefully the adopters or foster carers will carry on what was begun before placement; they might need guidance or only encouragement. But there may come a time when more intensive life story work is required or the therapeutic needs of the child become more acute.

Mandy was placed for adoption, aged four, with a simplified life story record that she could understand and loved having read to her. She was an easy child to bring up until she was 10. Then she suddenly truanted from school and attacked her adoptive parents. She dismissed her life story as a 'fairy story for stupid kids'. She was referred to a psycho-therapist who took her back to the beginning, and together they "recycled" her story to satisfy her greater curiosity and comprehension. As Mandy became a teenager, she continued to work with her therapist on her difficult narrative.

- **Speedy referrals to experts as and when required.** If a pathway to experts who may be required in the future is included in the placement support plan, many unnecessary crises could be avoided. Placements have disrupted because urgent referrals to education and health experts, to therapists or to specialist post-placement agencies, have led nowhere fast enough. A child might need private education or treatment in order for a placement to survive. To ensure a quick response before it is too late, both how to access a service, and how it will be funded, have to be established at the beginning. It may seem pessimistic to make arrangements for the worst scenario that everyone hopes will never happen, but we can think of it like a life insurance: we don't expect to die young just because we cover the eventuality.

- **Negotiating, supervising or managing contact arrangements.**
  Even if the significance of connection, the need for continuity and
  the purpose of contact have been agreed, most families and
  children will need support to manage and maintain the
  arrangements. It may be a matter of organising the practicalities of
  travel and venues or it may be that preparation and feedback are
  important for any one of the parties involved in direct contact.
  Indirect letterbox contact has to be carefully administered if it is to
  be meaningful for the child and both families.

*Birth families as well are likely to find difficulty in
knowing what to write, either to their children or to
the adoptive parents. Written agreements about
such matters go only so far; the parties to them may
need help in their realisation.*

(Department of Health, 1999, p 55)

- **Financial and practical assistance.** Some families can fight for
  everything they need but others cannot and would prefer to have
  a support worker who will fight for them. People who are good at
  bringing up children are not necessarily good at filling out forms,
  finding out about benefit changes or claiming what is their due. A
  welfare rights worker attached to the placement support team can
  guide carers who do not have the time and energy left at the end
  of the day to pick their way through complicated national and
  local authority allowance and grant systems.
  Having to deal with aids, adaptations, special equipment, an
  incontinence laundry service, or transport and wheelchair access
  can overwhelm carers of a disabled child and obscure the deeper
  issues in a permanent placement. 'I don't pay much attention to
  the social workers coming in and out, as long as the nappy service
  is working,' said an exhausted single adopter. Practical help of the
  right kind, at the right time, may pave the way for more
  therapeutic support work later.
  All agreements regarding allowances, grants and finance for

services in the future should leave permanent carers in no doubt about where the money will come from, and how it is to be paid. This is especially important in inter-agency placements or if the carers do not live in the area of the placing authority.

- **Health and education advice and guidance.** Children placed from care may have more than the average number of health and educational problems. Very often families are confused by medical assessments and opinions and they need a "medical interpreter" to explain what they have been told.

> *We had all these doctors asking questions, half of them we couldn't answer. They knew Matty was adopted but it didn't seem to make any difference. We got so flustered we couldn't really understand what they said about him.*
>
> (Adopter of child with genetic medical condition)

- **Education can make or break a placement.** The right school can be of immense support to adopters. But no available school or the wrong school can put a placement at risk. If carers do not agree with a Statement of Educational Needs, or if the child does not get a place in the school of their choice, carers may have to handle a long process of appeals. Including a named person in the placement support package to give educational advice, as and when required, can be a reassuring addition.
- **Short breaks as and how families want to use them.** Permanent carers often say, before a child is placed with them, that they will not want their child to have breaks away from home. But if the possibility and availability of short breaks is written into the support agreement, families will feel free to change their minds later.
It is essential to tailor short breaks to individual needs.

A couple who fostered three siblings under seven found it impossible to plan a year ahead as their local authority expected them to do. They wanted relief quickly when they most needed it.

In contrast, a single adopter of two children with Down's syndrome liked to feel that she could book holidays for herself knowing that the children would be looked after.

- **Training opportunities.** Study days and workshops for groups of carers are usually popular events in the placement support programme. Behaviour problems, attachment difficulties, adolescence and sexual development, special education, medical conditions, alternative treatments and welfare rights are among the topics most often requested. It is not always necessary to find an outside speaker; there may be enough expertise among carers to learn from each other.

One adoptive father was a reflexologist. He taught the other carers in the group how to make physical contact with defensive, distant children who avoided closeness. He demonstrated that gently massaging feet is not threatening and can begin to build trust between carers and child. At the same time, it is giving real, concentrated attention to the child, which is not the same as half listening while we peel the potatoes. All the people who attended this workshop, including the social workers, took away new ideas to put into practice.

We have to remember that many carers will not be able to come to training events unless their children can come too. Reliable child care or parallel events for children are therefore essential.

- **Regular reviews.** Circumstances change, needs change, carers as well as children grow older. Life stages such as starting school, adding more children to the family, divorce, moving house, children leaving home, retirement and death will have an impact on every member of the family and on their relationships with each other. Regular reviews of support services will make carers feel valued and ensure that the child's voice continues to be heard.

If this list of support needs sounds daunting for workers, we have to think how carers must feel, who have to grapple with all these issues on behalf of their child.

Many families have the commitment, the energy, and the imagination to meet the needs of children who have to be separated from their birth parents. Many children have enough resilience and courage to entrust themselves to new families. But we have no right to expect the resulting placements to be better than the support we give.

Further reading

Argent H (ed) (2003) *Models of Adoption Support*, London: BAAF

Argent H (2003) *Whatever Happened to Adam?*, London: BAAF

Department of Health (1999) *Adoption Now: Messages from research*, London: Department of Health

Lowe N, Murch M, Borkowsky M, Weaver A, Beckford V and Thomas C (1999) *Supporting Adoption: Reframing the approach*, London: BAAF

National Foster Care Association (1999) *UK National Standards for Foster Care*, London: NFCA

O'Neill C (2003) 'The simplicity and complexity of support' in Argent H (ed) *Models of Adoption Support*, London: BAAF

Rushton A and Dance C (2002) *Adoption Support Services for Families in Difficulty: A literature review and UK survey*, London: BAAF

Smith F and Brann C with Cullen D and Lane M (2004) *Fostering Now: Current law including regulations, guidance and standards (England)*, London: BAAF

Smith F and Stewart R with Cullen D (2006) *Adoption Now: Law, regulations, guidance and standards* (England), London: BAAF

For children

Foxon J (2004) *Nutmeg Gets a Little Help*, London: BAAF

TIP 8

Don't overlook the birth family

> *What kind of mother am I? I fought and lost and then gave in – I signed my children away. How do you live with that?*
>
> *(Charlton et al, 1998, p 46)*

The families of children who become looked after are not a powerful group. Many are socially disadvantaged and feel alienated from public services. Their contribution to their children's development is easily undervalued and undermined. We do not help children by disregarding their birth families.

Work with birth parents before, during, and after alternative family placement has to combine support, counselling, information, and advocacy. This task usually falls rather vaguely to the child's social worker, but it may be preferable to ensure that these services are provided by an outside agency: a voluntary agency or a lay advocate working with the parents' solicitor. Many birth parents are understandably resistant to working with their local authority if they are contesting a court case or are simply not in agreement with their child's placement. The National Minimum Standards for England and Wales require that birth parents will have access to a support worker independent of the child's social worker from the time adoption is identified as the plan for the child (Standard 7.4).

Unfortunately, it is too easy for birth families to be labelled as unco-operative if they do not welcome counselling to accept their loss, which is often all the local authority can offer, and which may not be altogether appropriate when parents are looking for advocacy, information and support. The sparse research available indicates that birth families, on the whole, do not experience the statutory services as supportive. Being seen as unco-operative can lead to the decision that direct contact would be disruptive or should be terminated.

Rob was placed in permanent foster care when he was nine years old. His mother's partner had allegedly abused Rob and was not allowed to accompany the mother to the weekly contact meetings in a local family centre, supervised by Rob's social worker. The mother, Rita, was unable to go anywhere on her own, and was duly collected and taken back home by taxi. Sometimes, when Rita was ill, she forgot to cancel the taxi or to warn the social workers that she would not be turning up. The meetings were reduced from weekly to monthly and then to four times a year.

After another year of increasingly stressful contact, Rob became hostile during Rita's visits and finally refused to go to the family centre. At the same time, his behaviour in the foster home seriously deteriorated. His social worker felt that Rita had spoilt every chance she had been given and was

> *now undermining Rob's excellent placement. He urged the local authority to apply for a termination of contact order*
>
> *(Section 34 of the 1989 Children Act)*

It was never likely that these contact arrangements would work. Rita had mild learning difficulties and agoraphobia. She needed preparation before each visit (information about Rob's progress, activities, interests), sympathetic support during the meetings with her son (approval, encouragement, respect), and an opportunity to talk about her feelings after each visit (pride in her child, grief and anger). Rob was confused by negative messages from his social worker and was communicating his distress about the unsatisfactory contact arrangements by his behaviour.

It seems strange to blame birth parents for not being able to deal with situations that would challenge the most competent among us. If they were as energetic, resourceful and reasonable, and as able to comply with arrangements and to co-operate with authority, as we might like them to be, then their children might not be living away from them in the first place.

What we have learned from birth families

- Losing a child remains a profound life factor; there are no "new starts" for birth parents and other close relatives. In a birth mother's group, one woman said that losing a child was like 'a ball and chain dragging behind you all your life', and another said it was like 'a life sentence without remission' (Jackson 2003, p 105). Some birth parents are stuck with their last view of their child.

> *He was standing by a window. 19th October. He kept crying out 'Mummy, Mummy'. It's always in my mind. It's always there, he's always crying. He was*

three years old for God's sake, three years old. It never goes away, it haunts me.

(Thoughts on adoption by birth mothers, Post Adoption Centre, London)

- Losing a child can be made worse by lack of adequate support and information or by severance of all contact with the child.
- Birth families from minority ethnic backgrounds who have to live with endemic racism may experience the loss of a child as further proof of discrimination.
- Birth parents who have a child taken away from them have to live with both social and legal judgements about their failure as parents. The adversarial nature of care proceedings focuses almost entirely on the weaknesses of birth families, without acknowledging their efforts or feelings. This "public shaming" can be particularly hard for families living in minority ethnic communities.
- There is no ritual to support birth families in their grief; no one sends flowers or calls to offer sympathy. Birth mothers, especially, often have to endure their loss alone. If the reality of the loss is not accepted, anger may become the only form of expression.
- Birth families have a continuing contribution to make to their children's lives if they are enabled to participate in plans, to negotiate the system, to accept the "non-parenting parent" role and to keep in touch, but lack of confidence and depression can prevent birth parents from playing an active role. 'I was left feeling flat and worthless but I do have something to offer them' (Birth Mother in Charlton *et al*, 1998, p 57).
- On the whole, birth parents do not want to disrupt placements or to distress their children. In her study of birth relatives with face-to-face contact, Neil (2003) found that uppermost in the minds of many was their wish not to cause any upset or to make any demands.
- Letterbox contact can be very difficult for birth families to establish and to maintain without ongoing support and guidance. Finding

the right words to communicate warmth without making claims is a challenge for all birth relatives.

- Birth mothers, in particular, need to know whether their child is safe and well, even when there is no other form of contact. Public disasters produce a deluge of enquiries; a tragedy involving children triggers anxieties for all parents, and birth parents should not be left to imagine the worst. 'I need to know if my child is all right. Is she dead or alive? If anything happens, would I get to know?' (birth mother in Charlton *et al*, 1998, p 55).

- If other birth children remain at home, they too will be affected by the loss of one or more siblings. Ideally, they ought to be offered a service in their own right – they need to understand the family story as much as absent children do. 'Hassan needs to see a picture of James so that Hassan can understand that James, the adopted child, didn't just disappear' (birth mother in Charlton *et al*, 1998, p 66).

- Birth parents find meeting with others who have had similar experiences both therapeutic and empowering. Successful groups have been set up by several agencies and have been co-led by social workers and women who have themselves lost a child to adoption. One birth mother wrote this poem about her experience of the group.

> Don't despair
> Elephants never forget
> We cry our tears of pain
> But we are always with you
> In the spirit of the day
> From one elephant to another.

(From *Elephants do cry* by Maria in *Thoughts on adoption by birth mothers in contested adoptions*, Post Adoption Centre)

A birth mother in a different group, who had relinquished her baby many years ago, wrote: 'By the end of the group I was able to acknowledge that my son is not four months old any more, he is 19, and I have taken steps to make it possible for him to contact me should he wish to do so' (Post Adoption Centre, 1990).

- The birth families of disabled children are generally burdened with a particularly heavy emotional load. They suffer a double loss: they mourn the child that might have been, and they grieve about the child they have relinquished or the child that was taken away. Birth siblings of disabled children who have been placed outside the family need special attention; they may carry both sorrow and guilt on behalf of their parents.

● Birth grandparents and other birth relatives may be able to offer invaluable continuity when children lose their parents.

> *We are the main steady line that has always been there…we've always been there and we always will be. You know, which I think all children need, they need at least someone that's gonna follow through from day one.*
>
> *(Grandparent with regular face-to-face contact in Neil and Howe, 2004, p 98)*

Family Group Conferences

Family Group Conferences (FGCs) originated in New Zealand as a method of involving the birth family when plans have to be made for a child's care and safety. They are based on the belief that the family network is aware of its own strengths and resources, as well as weaknesses, and knows best what goes on in the family. The role of the professional in FGCs is to facilitate the family decision-making process.

FGCs may be used successfully:

- to explore the possibility of placements with family or friends;
- to enhance the likelihood of rehabilitation with parents or within the kinship network;
- to make safe arrangements for continuity and contact;
- to promote positive partnerships between families and agencies;
- to empower people from minority ethnic groups who may have difficulty in dealing with a predominantly "other" organisation;
- to serve as a review mechanism for the birth family.

The Family Rights Group (see Useful Organisations) has developed a model for FGCs which many agencies now follow with good results. But there is no hard and fast rule about how kinship networks should be involved in making decisions. Any method that allows the extended birth family to be heard is good for children.

Further reading

Charlton L, Crank M, Kansara K and Oliver C (1998) *Still Screaming: Birth parents compulsorily separated from their children*, Manchester: After Adoption

Howe D, Sawbridge P and Hinings D (1992) *Half a Million Women: Mothers who lose their children through adoption*, London: Penguin

Jackson J (2003) 'The Nottingham Drop-In: providing mutual support for birth mothers' in Argent H (eds) *Staying Connected*, London: BAAF

Lindley B (1998) *Partnership with Birth Families in the Adoption Process*, London: Family Rights Group

Neil E (2003) 'Accepting the reality of adoption: birth relatives' experiences of face-to-face contact', *Adoption & Fostering,* 27:2, pp 32–43

Neil E and Howe D (eds) (2004) *Contact in Adoption and Permanent Foster Care*, London: BAAF

Post Adoption Centre Practice Paper (undated), *Thoughts on Adoption by Birth Mothers in Contested Adoptions*, London: Post Adoption Centre

Post Adoption Centre Discussion Paper (1990) *Groups for Women who have Parted with a Child for Adoption*, London: Post Adoption Centre

TIP 9

Promote openness

The meaning of openness

- Openness is a state of mind that should permeate every permanent placement. It is relatively easy to assess early on in the placement process whether there is openness in a family.

- Comments like: 'We'll always leave it to her to bring up the subject', or: 'I won't want to upset her by saying anything about her dad', are danger signals that need to be addressed, whereas: 'There's nothing you can't talk about', or: 'You've got to be really ready to listen' sound much more promising.

- Openness is not a static quality: it can develop to meet needs. An awareness of the value of openness to children can inspire families to create it.

- Openness is not a one-way process: communicative openness has to start with the workers who are recruiting and preparing families and with the way that departments and agencies communicate with each other and share information.

Scenario one

Linda's social workers, birth family, and adopters prided themselves on having achieved an "open adoption". The two families met twice a year in a theme park about halfway between their two homes. There was no contact between meetings; the adopters never spoke of the birth family and neither did Linda. The birth parents were informed of the dates of each meeting and sent travel vouchers by post.

Tensions rose in the adoptive household during the run-up to each meeting: Linda's behaviour at home and at school deteriorated and the adopters bickered with each other.

The adopters insisted on paying for everything and everybody at the theme park because they knew the birth family couldn't afford to; the local authority was pleased not to have to foot the bill.

During the meetings Linda was uncommunicative and visibly embarrassed. The birth parents felt inadequate and the adopters became irritated with what they saw as their wasted efforts. Both families were careful not to overstep some imaginary boundary but no one felt satisfied. Everyone was relieved when it was over for another six months. It usually took the adoptive family two weeks to return to "normal".

Scenario two

This was not an "open adoption". Face-to-face contact or any direct communication between Carl and his birth family could not be allowed for reasons of safety.

Letterbox contact was mediated by Children's Services. Carl's birth mother occasionally wrote to the adopters, with help from her independent social worker, and enclosed a postcard for Carl.

The adopters made a special folder with Carl to keep all his postcards in; they encouraged him to write cards back and talked about the news they might want to share with his birth mother. They answered all questions readily as well as truthfully. Carl felt on safe enough ground to say how angry his birth parents made him but that he loved them all the same. The openness in this family enabled Carl to keep his birth family in mind and his story in one piece.

David Brodzinsky (2006) compares "communicative openness" with "structural openness". Communicative openness may or may not lead to an open placement, but structural openness without communicative openness will cause stress and resentment.

In the first scenario above, the adults grudgingly observe an agreement to the letter, but compliance is unrelated to openness. Maintaining this kind of contact will eventually lead nowhere except to finding reasons to curtail or terminate it.

The second scenario leaves the door open for meaningful continuity and review arrangements to suit changing circumstances.

Optimum factors in openness

- Carers see positives in continuity for the child; they acknowledge that caring for children permanently is different from raising biological children.
- Birth parents have been included in decisions and support the placement; they accept that they still have a significant part to play.
- The child hears the same story from both sets of parents.

Openness is a prerequisite for all the other tips in this book to be effective. Without communicative openness, work with children and families will be put in jeopardy. With communicative openness, the disruption of many placements may be averted.

Further reading

Brodzinsky D (2006) 'Reconceptualising openness in adoption: Implications from research and practice' in Brodzinsky D and Palacios J (eds) *Psychological Issues in Adoption: Theory, research, and practice*, Westport, CT: Greenwood

TIP 10

Don't fear failure

Adapted from *Dealing with Disruption*, (Argent and Coleman, 2006)

A fear of failure always lurks just below the surface of family placement work: a false expectation of a 100 per cent success rate may deter carers from seeking help if placement difficulties arise.

Few of us like to risk denting the applicants' confidence by sounding a negative note at the beginning, but it is important that the less happy side of family placement is acknowledged and that children are also helped to understand that we can't get it right every time.

> *If a placement disrupts, it is never the result of what one party has done or left undone.*
>
> *It is usually a combination of:*
>
> - *unidentified circumstances*

- *misinterpreted circumstances*

- *unpredictable circumstances*

(Donley, 1981)

The word "disruption", in preference to the more pejorative term "breakdown", was first used by Kay Donley to describe the unplanned ending of a family placement in the early 1970s. 'When there is a disruption, there is a family crisis' said Donley at a conference organised by BAAF (then ABAFA) in 1975. It is perhaps appropriate to go further now, and to maintain that disruption is a part of the family placement process, and that an awareness of disruption should be built into the training and preparation of all permanent carers.

Although outcomes for children placed young are still very good, and for later placed children still very much 'worth the risk' (Rushton, 2003), some permanent placements will inevitably disrupt. It should not be a matter of failing or succeeding as carers, but of being given the tools to manage and the support to withdraw if and when it is no longer possible to manage.

Common causes of disruption

- Incomplete or unshared information about the child, the carers or the birth family – possibly due to a well-intentioned but misguided attempt to present a positive picture.
- Inaccurate assessment of children's attachment patterns and continuity needs, including their relationship with previous carers.
- Changes in the family lifestyle and career status; sickness, death, divorce, pregnancy, or redundancy.
- Post-placement depression, if the emotional rewards are not as anticipated; like post-natal depression, this can be a seriously debilitating condition, which may be masked by more obvious problems in a placement.
- Failure of health, education, and therapeutic services to meet an expected or unexpected need.

- Poor inter-agency and inter-departmental communication, which can cause confusion for the child, the carers and the workers.

> *There were people coming in and out, telling us different things and giving us different advice. We never truly knew who was doing what and I don't think they did either. It was like the right hand not knowing what the left was doing.*
>
> *(Prospective adopter at disruption meeting)*

- Not enough consideration of carers' own children's needs and perspectives, or of the age of the fostered or adopted child in relation to the carers' birth children.
- Lack of clarity or agreement about either the purpose or the management of contact.
- Inadequate placement support; ignoring the danger signals.

> *A single potential permanent carer complained that the placement disrupted because she had been unsupported. The social workers were horrified and said that they had visited more often than necessary because they knew the placement was at risk. 'That's right,' said the carer, 'but you always made me feel you were coming to check up, not to support me'.*

- A lack of openness in the carers' family.
- Not enough preparation of the child or children for the move to permanence, which may seem a threatening idea denoting a more final severance from the birth family.
- Not enough preparation of the carers to parent this particular child or group of children.

It will immediately be evident that the above list is just a different way of presenting the nine previous Tips. But it is a fact that, in spite of the most careful preparation, assessments, and training, in spite of shared information, experience, and knowledge, it is not possible to anticipate exactly what will happen when *this* child is placed with *this* family. Often we stand by and watch in respectful admiration as children and carers make the most precarious placements last. But we also have to stand by while seemingly promising placements crumble. As more and more older children with complex profiles need alternative families, it is predictable that the numbers of disruptions will rise.

Managing disruption

Dealing with disruption should be considered as an integral part of family placement services. How disruptions are managed needs to be enshrined in policy.

- Will there be a meeting with all concerned, to decide how the placement might be saved or to plan an ending? It is vital to identify whether the crisis is a cry for help or a plea for closure.
- Will there be an intensive period of preparation for disruption? Disruptions should be as carefully orchestrated as introductions.
- Will every effort be made to return the child to previous carers? It may be better for the child to share a bedroom than to face more strangers.
- Is the agency able to make priority arrangements for school, health, and therapy transfers? A break in essential services can constitute an added loss for a child.
- How will the birth family be involved? Changing circumstances may offer new opportunities for birth families to contribute to care plans.
- If two agencies are concerned, who will do what? If there is clarity and transparency, there will be fewer hard feelings.
- How will support and continuity be maintained for the child and the family after disruption? If children and families can't live together, it does not necessarily mean that there is no value in staying in touch.
- How soon after a disruption will there be a disruption meeting? A convenor has to be appointed to invite an independent Chair, to agree who will be asked to attend, to organise a venue and co-ordinate arrangements.

Disruption meetings

The purpose of disruption meetings

1. To enable participants to share information and feelings about the placement process without assigning blame.
2. To identify factors that have led to the disruption.
3. To interpret the current needs of the child, the carer, the birth family and the agency or agencies.
4. To formulate future plans for the child based on what has been learned from the disruption.
5. To highlight areas for development in policy and practice.

When?

Everyone needs time after a disruption to reflect on what has happened, but they also need to retain a clear memory of the chain of events.

How long?

It usually takes a whole day for everyone to be able to say what should be said, to know that they have been heard and to listen to everyone else. There has to be time to digress, to reconsider, to recall and to be upset.

Where?

A warm, light room with comfortable chairs, informally arranged, will generally give a reassuring message. It is preferable not to meet in local authority offices. Hot and cold drinks and a sandwich lunch in the meeting room should help to keep the momentum going.

Who?

If children are to participate, they need careful preparation; they will have to be fully aware of their own history as well as the purpose and structure of the meeting. It may be preferable for the Chair to organise the agenda so that the child attends for only part of the day or joins the meeting during the lunch break. Some children choose to stay away but want to send a letter, like Rob.

> **Dear meeting**
>
> *I am very sorry I cant live with Sue and Gery. I want to have a family but I want to stay in my foster home. I don't want to go to a diferent town. I like Sue and Gerry but I cant be good for them. I cant help it I was reely bad for them. I hurt the dog. I screamed in the nite, I just want to scream if I have to move again. I miss Sue and Gery lots and I want to keep seeing my Mum and big brother and I wish I cud see my dad.*
>
> *Yours sincerely*
> *Rob Oliver*

If children do not attend, who will speak for them? And if the child is black, where will the cultural competence come from?

Everyone who has been involved before, during, and after the placement should be invited to contribute. If anyone wishes to bring a friend or outside support worker they should be able to do so, but if there are child protection concerns, the Chair should always adopt the safest course.

Reports and minutes

As with any social work intervention, a full record should be made of disruption meetings by a skilled minute taker. An interpretative overview report with recommendations should be produced by the Chair of the meeting and circulated to the participants and to the panels that were involved in the placement. It is most important that the child's views are clearly recorded.

Learning from disruption

In order to disseminate what has been learnt from disruption, joint training might be offered to managers, practitioners and panel members to consider measures for preventing disruption in the future. It is as important to understand why some placements do not work as it is to rejoice that so many do.

> **However painful the process of disruption inevitably is, it can be viewed as a stage on the path to stability for the child and no one need lose everything.**
>
> (Argent, 2003, p 321)

Further reading

Argent H (ed) (2003) *Models of Adoption Support*, London: BAAF

Argent H and Coleman J (2006) *Dealing with Disruption*, London: BAAF

Donley K (1981) 'Further observations on disruption', in *Adoption Disruptions*, Washington DC: US Department of Health and Human Services

Fitzgerald J (1983, 1990) *Understanding Disruption*, London: BAAF

Rushton A (2003) *The Adoption of Looked After Children: A scoping review of research*, London: Social Care Institute of Excellence

Smith S (1994) *Learning from Disruption*, London: BAAF

Endpiece

This book should end as it began: in the firm belief that children can be successfully joined with a new family if they need one. So the last words about family placement must go to a child.

> *Me and my sister and brother, we live with our foster mum and dad. They haven't got no other kids so they love us like special. We're staying here for ever 'cause even grown ups can have families. We've got two families , we live with one and the other's like a spare.*
>
> *(Eight-year-old girl in permanent placement)*

Useful organisations

Adoption Register for England and Wales
Unit 4, Pavilion Business Park
Royds Hall Road
Wortley, Leeds LS12 6AJ
Tel: 0870 750 2176
www.adoptionregister.org.uk

Adoption UK
46 The Green
South Bar Street
Banbury OX16 9AB
Tel: 01295 752 240
www.adoptionuk.org

British Association for Adoption & Fostering (BAAF) and Be My Parent
Head Office
Saffron House
6–10 Kirby Street
London EC1N 8TS
Tel: 020 7421 2600
mail@baaf.org.uk
www.baaf.org.uk

BAAF Scotland
40 Shandwick Place
Edinburgh EH2 4RT
Tel: 0131 220 4749

BAAF Cymru
7 Cleeve House
Lambourne Crescent
Cardiff CF14 5GP
Tel: 029 2074 7934

BAAF Northern Ireland
Botanic House
1–5 Botanic Avenue
Belfast BT7 1JG
Tel: 028 9031 5494

Children 1st
83 Whitehouse Lane
Edinburgh EH9 1AT
Tel: 0131 446 2300
www.children1st.org.uk

Family Rights Group
The Print House
18 Ashwin Court
London E8 3DL
Tel: 020 7923 2628
www.frg.org.uk

Fostering Network
87 Blackfriars Road
London SE1 8HA
Tel: 020 7620 6400
www.fostering.net

Fostering Network Scotland
Ingram House, 2nd Floor
Glasgow G1 1DA
Tel: 0141 204 1400

Fostering Network Wales
Suite 11, 2nd Floor
Bay Chambers
West Bute Street
Cardiff Bay CF10 5BB
Tel: 029 2044 0940